Millionaire Landlord Chronicles:

Hilarious Stories and Proven Strategies for Tenant Management

Jason A Scott

Table of Content

Acknowledgment

I am immensely grateful for the completion of this book, and I would like to extend my heartfelt appreciation to the following individuals whose support, encouragement, and expertise made this journey possible:

First and foremost, I want to express my deepest gratitude to my dad, whose unwavering love and understanding allowed me to immerse myself in the writing process. Your constant encouragement and belief in my abilities have been a driving force behind the completion of this book.

I wholeheartedly express my gratitude to both my past and current tenants, whose interactions and experiences have presented valuable challenges that allowed me to grow and evolve.

To my esteemed colleagues and friends, thank you for the stimulating discussions, constructive feedback, and camaraderie throughout this endeavor. Your diverse perspectives enriched the content and kept me motivated during challenging times.

I would like to acknowledge the support of EditMojo for providing the editing and formatting of this book. Also, the book cover was designed by pch.vector / Freepik. Your assistance has been indispensable in bringing this project to fruition.

Lastly, I want to express my gratitude to my readers, whose interest and curiosity in this subject matter inspire me to continue exploring new avenues of knowledge.

This book would not have been possible without the collective contributions and encouragement of each one of you. Your presence in my life has been a blessing, and I am sincerely thankful for your support.

With heartfelt appreciation,

Jason A Scott

Introduction:

Welcome to the thrilling and uproarious world of landlording! Prepare yourself for a wild ride as we delve into the realm of rental properties, where each day unveils a delightful blend of surprises, challenges, and triumphs. Get ready to experience the highs and lows, the laughs and the shocks, as I take you on a personal journey through my incredible tenure as a landlord for the past 15 years.

Imagine having over 100 tenants, each with unique quirks and personalities, demanding your attention monthly. It's like managing a colorful circus, where the clowns and tightrope walkers never fail to entertain! And believe me; I've got stories that will make you double over with laughter and wonder how I kept my sanity intact.

Let me share a particularly memorable tale from my landlord adventures. Picture this: a tenant comes storming into my office, frantic and red-faced, insisting their mischievous dog devoured their rent money. I raised an eyebrow in disbelief. A dog with an appetite for cash? I had heard it all. After a moment of skepticism, I composed myself and tried to offer a sympathetic ear. "Well," I said, trying to stifle a chuckle, "I guess that's one way to avoid paying rent!"

But it's not all amusing anecdotes and zany characters. Being a landlord is a juggling act that requires serious dedication and a knack for problem-solving. I've faced my fair share of challenges, from negotiating with vendors who think they can charge an arm and a leg for simple repairs to dealing with tenants who believe paying rent is merely a suggestion. It can be a test of patience and wit, but it's also taught me invaluable life lessons.

What started as a simple rant about the challenges of being a landlord quickly transformed into an exploration of personal growth and mental fortitude. Those difficult tenants who tested my patience and resolve unwittingly became catalysts for my success. But navigating the murky waters of property management requires more than just a firm hand—it demands the ability to find humor in the absurd and the resilience to keep going even when things seem impossible.

Now, with many years of experience under my belt, I can handle everything with ease. I have developed an arsenal of strategies and tricks that have transformed my once chaotic workload into a well-oiled machine. Gone are the days of sleepless nights and endless phone calls. I have learned to delegate, streamline processes, and focus on my well-being. And getting a full night's sleep feels like winning the lottery!

Hold on tight as we embark on an exhilarating journey through the highs and lows of the rental business in this book. I'm excited to share the valuable lessons I've picked up over the years, earned through a mix of challenges, successes, blunders, and triumphs. But don't worry, it won't be a snooze-fest of dry advice and boring jargon. I'm here to entertain as much as educate!

As you read along, you'll find a conclusion at the end of each chapter. These conclusions are like little golden nuggets, encapsulating the core lessons I've learned from my experiences. They're not just random thoughts; they're the rental principles I'll passionately follow, born out of my challenges, mistakes, and newfound wisdom.

By sharing my crazy stories and hard-earned knowledge, I hope to provide valuable insights to my fellow landlords. Together, we can raise the bar of property management and create a community of successful and savvy landlords. And trust me, it won't be a lonely journey. This book is your ticket to laughs, tears, and unforgettable moments in the rental world.

So, fasten your seatbelts and enjoy the ride! Whether you're a seasoned landlord or a newbie, there's something here for everyone. And who knows, you might even learn a trick or two to save you from a dog-eaten rent emergency! Happy reading!

Chapter 1:
A Hands-On Landlord's Tale

Once upon a time, in a bustling cityscape where dreams intersected with reality, I found myself in the throes of managing my empire of apartments. While some landlords may rely on property management companies to lighten their load, I took the road less traveled, becoming a hands-on maestro of all things property-related. From juggling maintenance requests to scouting for exceptional tenants, crafting enticing advertisements to crafting budgets, my days were a whirlwind of excitement and responsibility.

But amid this whirlwind, I discovered the most fascinating part of my job lay in human interaction. Yes, dear readers, it was the tenants themselves who added that extra dash of flavor to my landlording journey. Each tenant came with unique quirks, tales, and occasional moments of perplexity. As I delved deeper into this intricate dance of landlord-tenant relationships, I realized that the key to success lived not only in bricks and mortar but in the art of communication and the power of the right mindset.

Establishing and maintaining open communication channels with tenants is imperative when managing rental properties. However, it is essential to acknowledge that mastering the art of conveying the right message and treating tenants in a way that resonates with their specific needs and preferences is a skill honed through experience and practice.

Each tenant brings their distinct habits, personality traits, and communication styles to the table. Understanding and adapting to these unique characteristics requires time and keenly observing their behaviors and preferences. Through this dedicated effort, property managers can develop a deep understanding of each tenant's individuality, including their habits, preferences, and preferred methods of communication.

By investing the time and energy to get to know your tenants, you gain invaluable insights into how best to engage with them effectively. Once you understand, you can tailor your communication approach to their needs and expectations. This personalized approach fosters trust, enhances tenant satisfaction, and cultivates a positive landlord-tenant relationship.

Developing open lines of communication with tenants is crucial, but it goes hand in hand with cultivating the right landlord mindset. Managing a property involves navigating many personalities and facing various positive and negative challenges. Treating property management as a business endeavor and maintaining a professional approach is vital to effectively handle these situations.

Adopting the right mindset entails recognizing that personal emotions should not interfere with day-to-day operations. It is natural to encounter ups and downs while managing a property, but it is important not to take things personally. Instead, view it as an opportunity to learn and grow. Mistakes are inevitable along the way, and it is crucial not to become upset or dwell on them excessively.

When faced with challenges or setbacks, it is essential to remain calm and ask yourself, "What can I do now?" This proactive approach ensures that you focus on finding solutions and acting rather than succumbing to frustration or dwelling on past errors. Adopting an action-oriented mindset empowers you to overcome obstacles and generate tangible results.

Remember that property management is a dynamic field requiring constant adaptation and learning. Embrace the journey as an opportunity for personal and professional growth. By maintaining a business-oriented mindset, refraining from taking things personally, and approaching challenges with a problem-solving attitude, you can navigate the complexities of property management effectively.

In conclusion, open communication with tenants is crucial, but it is equally important to cultivate the right mindset as a landlord. Treating property management as a business endeavor, remaining objective, and refraining from becoming disheartened by mistakes are key to developing a successful approach. By staying calm, taking proactive steps, and finding solutions, you can tackle challenges head-on and create a thriving rental environment.

Chapter 2:
The Overwhelming To-Do Lists

"That's so much to do!"

Let's dive into a common challenge that plagues us all: the never-ending to-do list. We've all been there, overwhelmed by the sheer number of tasks clamoring for our attention. From finding new tenants to dealing with repairs, managing notices to promoting our properties, it feels like we're lost in a maze of responsibilities. But fear not, my friend, for I'm here to share a life-saving strategy that will revolutionize how you tackle your overwhelming to-do lists. Get ready to unleash the power of the 80/20 method!

Imagine this scenario: I, as a landlord, face an enormous pile of tasks. It's enough to make anyone feel like they're drowning in responsibilities. But instead of succumbing to the chaos, I decided to be strategic. I hatch a plan to conquer the overwhelming onslaught that threatened to consume me.

Enter the 80/20 method—a clever approach focusing on getting the most results with the least effort. The 80/20 method, also known as the "Pareto Principle," is attributed to the Italian economist and sociologist Vilfredo Pareto (1848-1923). This principle is derived from his studies on income distribution and wealth in society. Pareto observed that approximately 80% of the land in Italy was owned by 20% of the population. This observation led him to propose the general principle that a significant portion of results, outputs, or consequences are often determined by a small number of causes or inputs.

In business and management, the 80/20 principle suggests that 80% of the results or outcomes are typically generated by 20% of the efforts or inputs. It's also applied in various contexts, such as time management, where 80% of results come from 20% of activities, or product sales, where 80% of revenue comes from 20% of customers or products.

The Pareto Principle has proven to be a valuable concept in decision-making and resource allocation, as it allows individuals and organizations to focus on the most impactful areas and prioritize their efforts accordingly. By identifying the vital few factors that drive the majority of results, one can optimize their efficiency and effectiveness in various aspects of life and work.

So, how does it apply to task and time management? It's pretty simple. Picture having a list of ten important things that need your attention. Instead of feeling overwhelmed by the sheer volume, I prioritized the two tasks that would give me 80% of the desired outcomes.

My goal wasn't just about checking items off a list. It was about maximizing the financial returns on my efforts. By focusing on the tasks that would make the biggest impact, I ensured that my time and energy were spent where it mattered. It was like discovering a secret superpower that transformed me from an overwhelmed landlord into a productivity wizard.

But here's the best part: the magic of the 80/20 method doesn't stop there. Every day, armed with a fresh list of ten crucial tasks, I tackled the battle of productivity head-on. Once again, I carefully selected the two tasks that would bring me closer to my ultimate goal of financial success. And so, the cycle continued—a constant quest for prioritization that kept chaos at bay and propelled me forward, one step at a time.

Let's inject some humor into this tale—a funny interlude celebrating the never-ending list. Imagine me, the brave landlord, facing my arch-nemesis with determination in my eyes. Armed with my trusty 80/20 sword, I sliced through the overwhelming tasks with finesse. Repair requests quivered in fear, notices trembled at my sight, and advertisements bowed down to my strategic prowess. Each successful task became a victory, inching me closer to triumph, knowing I had vanquished the beast, one task at a time.

In conclusion, my friend, let's reflect on the valuable lessons this tale imparts. Conquering overwhelming to-do lists isn't about doing everything at once—it's about prioritization. Embrace the power of the 80/20 method and witness how chaos transforms into clarity, stress fades away, and exhaustion gives way to efficiency. So, as you embark on your journey as a landlord, remember this: it's not about how many tasks you complete but how wisely you choose them.

Chapter 3:
Secrets of Maximizing Returns

"So many applicants, but who will be the right tenant?"

Welcome, my fellow adventurers, to the exhilarating world of tenant applications—a dazzling spectacle that can leave even the most seasoned landlords pondering the age-old question: "How on earth am I going to review all these applications?" Fear not, for I, your trusty guide, am here to reveal the secrets of successfully navigating this intricate tango. Get ready to embark on a journey where good tenants are discovered, vacancies are filled, and the harmonious melody of your landlord-tenant relationship flourishes.

As the month draws to a close, the 25th day arrives, and with it, a whirlwind of tenant applications descends upon us like a flock of seagulls descending upon a scrumptious French fry. Our goal is clear: to achieve maximum occupancy with zero vacancies. The pressure mounts, and we grapple with a crucial question—how can we make the right decisions without succumbing to hasty choices?

In the exciting realm of landlording, we must embrace the reality that finding the ideal tenant may require time and patience. Discovering the perfect match could take a month, two, or even three. So, my fellow adventurers, let us resist the allure of desperation and remain steadfast. A good tenant pays rent promptly and rarely bombards us with complaints.

Through personal experience, I've learned that accepting tenants out of sheer desperation or only to fill a vacancy often leads to regret. The hours spent dealing with problematic tenants or enduring the grueling eviction process can take a toll on our precious time and hard-earned finances. It becomes clear that the price we pay for hastily filling a vacancy is far greater than any temporary loss resulting from a vacant unit. Time, dear friends, is a valuable resource that demands wise allocation within our business.

In this revelation, I discovered the secret to maximizing our return on investment—the meticulous review of potential tenant applications. This, my friends, is the pinnacle of our landlord tasks, the crème de la crème. It's akin to handpicking a star basketball player during the NBA draft. Just as the right selection can make or break a team, choosing the right tenant can be the deciding factor in a harmonious landlord-tenant relationship.

Now, let us pause momentarily and indulge in a whimsical interlude—a playful journey into the imaginary realm of the Court of Tenant Applications. Envision yourself, my dear adventurers, as the esteemed commissioner of a landlord's basketball league, comfortably seated in your luxurious armchair. Before you, an expansive basketball court materializes, filled with a sea of tenant applications. Each application takes the form of a player eagerly vying for a spot on your team. With a keen eye, you observe their moves, assess their statistics, and unleash your intuition to determine who has the potential to become the MVP of your rental property.

As our whimsical interlude draws to a close, the review of tenant applications takes center stage, demanding our utmost attention and care. In our quest for the perfect match, let us resist the enticing call of desperation. Instead, focus on finding tenants who bring harmony, reliability, and peace to our properties—a harmonious melody that transforms our rental properties into havens of contentment.

So, my fellow adventurers, remember to savor the journey as you navigate the thrilling dance of tenant applications. Embrace the excitement, laughter, and occasional challenges that come your way. Trust your instincts, take your time, and remain steadfast in pursuing the perfect tenant. And when you find them, rejoice knowing that your patience and careful consideration have paid off. Let us create a symphony of success where our properties thrive and our landlord-tenant relationships flourish.

Chapter 4:
Finding the Right Tenant

"You are telling me something different than what you have on the application."

Choosing the right tenant is a crucial step in the landlording journey. Once I hand over the keys and they take possession of the property, I lose all leverage and control. That's why it's vital to carefully evaluate tenant applications and be on the lookout for red flags. In this chapter, I will share my personal experiences and insights on what to look for in tenant applications. So, grab a cup of coffee and join me on this enlightening journey that might just save you a bunch of headaches!

When reviewing an application, the first thing that catches my attention is any blank spaces or missing information. If Carlos leaves the section where he is supposed to fill out his current residence and contact information for his existing landlord empty, it raises some concerns. It suggests that either he didn't give notice to his current landlord, or he doesn't have a good relationship with them. These blanks can indicate potential problems down the road, so it's crucial not to overlook them.

As all my properties are pet-free communities, I employ a clever strategy to uncover whether applicants have pets or not. Instead of directly asking if they have dogs, for example, I include a question like, "How many dogs do you have?" This subtle approach allows me to "trick" them into revealing the truth. If an applicant mentions having dogs despite knowing that it's a pet-free community, it immediately raises a red flag and prompts further investigation.

Upon receiving tenant applications via email, I always take the time to give them a call. This personal interaction serves multiple purposes. First and foremost, it allows me to hear their voice, which can provide valuable insights into their character and honesty. As Judge Judy says on her show, "You don't need to have a good memory if you just tell the truth." By asking them the same questions that are already included in the application, I can assess if their answers remain consistent. Most people don't remember every detail they put on the application, so if their responses align with what they wrote, it increases the likelihood that they are being truthful. On the other hand, inconsistencies or evasive answers raise doubts and indicate that further scrutiny is necessary.

While reviewing applications and speaking with potential tenants, I've learned to trust my gut instinct. There have been instances where everything seemed fine on paper, but something in my intuition told me to proceed with caution. In one memorable case, a prospective tenant seemed perfect on paper—steady income, good references, and a seemingly pleasant demeanor. However, during our phone conversation, there was something in the tone of their voice that raised my suspicions. It's difficult to pinpoint exactly what triggered my gut feeling, but I decided to follow it. A quick online search revealed a trail of negative reviews and legal disputes related to their previous tenancies. Trusting my intuition prevented a potentially disastrous situation and saved me from future headaches.

In the landlording world, tenant screening is an art. It's about going beyond the surface and looking for signs that may not be immediately apparent. It's about paying attention to the details, trusting your instincts, and conducting thorough due diligence. Each tenant application is like a puzzle piece, and by carefully examining and piecing them together, you can create a complete picture of the applicant.

So, my fellow adventurers in the realm of landlording, remember to read tenant applications with care. Look out for blanks, use clever questions to uncover hidden information, and follow up with phone calls to assess consistency and trustworthiness. Above all, trust your gut instincts—it's a powerful tool in making informed decisions. By employing these strategies, you'll be well on your way to finding the right tenants who will contribute to the success and harmony of your rental properties.

Chapter 5:
Trust but Verify

"Knowing what you know now, would you..."

As I delve into the intriguing world of tenant screening, I reflect on the importance of thorough investigation and verification. The tenant application serves as a window into the potential tenant's history, and my duty as a responsible landlord is to scrutinize every detail with precision and care. With that in mind, I have established a comprehensive set of inquiries to gather vital information about the applicant's employment history, residential background, and character references.

On the tenant application form that I provide, I include sections that require applicants to disclose their employment history for the past five years, as well as their previous residential addresses during that same timeframe. Additionally, I request the contact information of their direct supervisors and past landlords. This collection of data serves as the foundation for my tenant screening process, providing valuable insights into an applicant's reliability, stability, and overall suitability as a tenant.

When reviewing the applications, I meticulously examine the employment section. I look for consistency and longevity in job tenure, as these qualities often indicate a level of commitment and financial stability. However, it is crucial to go beyond the information provided on paper. I believe in the power of personal connection, so I take the extra step of reaching out to the applicant's current employer to obtain a firsthand perspective on their work ethic and professionalism.

During one such call, I vividly recall speaking with a supervisor who seemed eager to share their thoughts on the applicant. As I delved into the conversation, I posed a simple yet revealing question: "If given the choice, would you choose to retain this employee?" The supervisor's response was nothing short of enlightening. With a hearty chuckle, they confessed that the applicant's dedication, punctuality, and overall performance had positively impacted the team. Their genuine enthusiasm left no room for doubt—I had stumbled upon a promising candidate whose work ethic and reliability aligned with my expectations as a discerning landlord.

Moving on to the residential history section, I find myself reminiscing about a particularly memorable encounter with an applicant's supposed landlord. Armed with the contact information provided, I dialed the number with a mix of anticipation and curiosity. However, much to my surprise, the person who answered the call seemed unaware of their role as a landlord. Confusion permeated the conversation as they fumbled through basic questions about rent amounts and the number of bedrooms in the alleged rental unit. It became evident that this "landlord" was nothing more than a family member or friend attempting to deceive me. In that moment, I couldn't help but chuckle at the audacity of such a ploy. The applicant's dishonesty, as revealed by this humorous encounter, served as an unequivocal red flag. It affirmed the necessity of thorough verification and the importance of upholding integrity throughout the tenant screening process.

While contacting current landlords can be insightful, I have come to recognize that some may be hesitant to provide direct answers. Fear of potential legal liabilities often hinders landlords from divulging comprehensive information. However, I have devised a clever strategy to bypass this hurdle. Rather than pressing for specific details, I ask a simple yet revealing question: "Knowing what you know now, would you rent to this applicant again?" This question elicits a candid response, allowing the existing landlord to express their overall satisfaction or dissatisfaction with the tenant. Their answer speaks volumes, guiding me in my decision-making process.

Throughout my years of experience, I have learned the importance of verifying every single detail provided on the applicant's form. It is a task that requires patience, persistence, and a keen eye for discrepancies. I refuse to make exceptions if any inconsistency arises during my conversations with employers or landlords. Maintaining a rigorous and fair screening process is crucial for protecting my investment and fostering a trustworthy and harmonious landlord-tenant relationship.

In conclusion, the tenant screening process is an art that demands attention to detail, resourcefulness, and a dash of humor. By meticulously investigating the applicant's employment history, reaching out to references, and verifying every piece of information, I can ensure that my rental properties are entrusted to responsible and reliable tenants. Through anecdotes and real-life encounters, I have shared the humorous and enlightening moments shaping my approach to tenant screening. As I continue on this ever-evolving journey as a landlord, I remain committed to upholding the highest standards of integrity, fairness, and thoroughness in the pursuit of finding exceptional tenants who will care for and respect the homes they inhabit.

Chapter 6:
Red Flags

"I am not your tour guide..."

As I delve deeper into the intricate world of tenant screening, I find myself reflecting on the importance of selecting the right tenant—a decision that can make or break my rental business. With every rental property I own, I understand that finding reliable and responsible tenants is paramount to achieving long-term success. As such, I have learned to devote more time and attention to this critical aspect of landlording. Before we embark on this enlightening journey together, it is crucial to reiterate that The Fair Housing Act prohibits any form of discrimination based on race, color, national origin, religion, sex (including gender identity and sexual orientation), familial status, and disability. Upholding the principles of fairness and equality is not only a legal obligation but also a moral imperative that I hold dear. So, as I share with you five types of applicants I often reject and the reasoning behind my decisions, let us embrace the spirit of inclusivity and compassion in all our interactions.

First and foremost, let us address the issue of out-of-towners. While the prospect of new tenants moving to the area can be exciting, it can also be accompanied by a flurry of questions and requests for guidance. These individuals, in their quest for knowledge about the neighborhood, nearby amenities, and schools, often seek to extract every ounce of information from me. However, I have come to realize that my time is a valuable and finite resource. Every minute spent on the phone with an inquisitive potential tenant could be better utilized in more productive endeavors. What's more, I have noticed that the majority of these lengthy conversations rarely result in an actual rental agreement. Hence, I have learned to graciously redirect these eager individuals to other sources of information, allowing them to navigate their relocation journey independently.

Moving on, let us discuss the matter of lease term duration. As a landlord, I prefer stability and continuity in my rental properties. Therefore, I am inclined to seek tenants committed to a minimum lease term of twelve months. This longer duration not only helps reduce turnover and the associated costs but also fosters a sense of community and permanence among the tenants. Shorter lease terms, akin to temporary arrangements, tend to disrupt the flow and predictability of my rental business. Consequently, I gently guide those seeking shorter-term leases towards alternative housing options catering to their needs.

Now, let us focus on a characteristic that raises a proverbial red flag during the tenant screening process—defensiveness. When engaging in a preliminary phone conversation with potential tenants, it is natural to ask a few questions to ascertain their suitability for the rental property. However, if an applicant displays an overly defensive or confrontational attitude in response to these inquiries, it gives rise to concerns. Such behavior may indicate an unwillingness to provide honest and transparent information or a propensity for difficult and contentious interactions. As I strive to maintain a harmonious landlord-tenant relationship, I find it prudent to prioritize individuals who approach these initial conversations with openness and a willingness to engage in productive dialogue.

Moving swiftly along, let us explore the curious case of fast talkers. There is an old adage that suggests "talk is cheap," and in the realm of tenant screening, it is a sentiment I hold close to my heart. When confronted with a potential tenant who rattles off their responses at an accelerated pace, I cannot help but raise an eyebrow. Experience has taught me that such rapid-fire speech may serve as a camouflage for concealed intentions or a clever ploy to divert attention from potential concerns. Therefore, I have honed my ability to listen attentively, sifting through the verbal flurry to identify any inconsistencies or hidden messages. The speed at which someone communicates may reveal much about their character and intentions, prompting me to exercise caution when proceeding with the application process.

Finally, let us address the matter of applicants who make requests for special favors even before they have secured a rental agreement. It is common for potential tenants to seek flexibility or accommodations. However, when faced with applicants who ask to make payment arrangements for move-in costs or seek exceptions to established policies, I find myself raising an incredulous eyebrow. It is essential to maintain a fair and consistent approach in my business dealings, treating all applicants equally and adhering to established protocols. If an individual is unable to meet the standard move-in requirements, such as paying the full month's rent and a deposit equivalent to 1.5 times the monthly rent, it raises doubts about their financial stability and responsibility. As a responsible landlord, it is my duty to prioritize applicants who demonstrate the ability to fulfill their financial obligations without resorting to special arrangements.

These anecdotes and observations are intended to shed light on the nuances and complexities of tenant screening. It is important to note that every landlord possesses their unique set of criteria and preferences when selecting tenants. What may serve as a red flag for one landlord may be inconsequential to another. Nonetheless, as we navigate the intricacies of this process, let us strive to maintain fairness, transparency, and adherence to legal obligations. By doing so, we can ensure a rental business that flourishes and fosters positive and respectful relationships between landlords and tenants.

Now, my fellow adventurers in the landlording realm, armed with a sense of humor and self-awareness, let us embark on our quest to find reliable, responsible, and respectful tenants. May we navigate the winding path of tenant screening with wisdom, integrity, and an unwavering commitment to fairness. Together, let us create a harmonious and prosperous rental business that stands as a testament to the power of good tenant selection practices.

Chapter 7:
Desperate Tenant

"But I can pay you 6 months' rent in advance if you let me move in today."

Oh, the audacity of some potential tenants! There's a saying in the landlording world: "If it sounds too good to be true, it probably is." And boy, did I learn that lesson the hard way when I encountered the enigmatic Tony.

Picture this: I was knee-deep in the search for a new tenant for my cozy two-bedroom unit. The phone rang, and on the other end was Tony, a smooth talker with a story that raised my eyebrows. He had a decent job, or so he claimed, but when I asked for employment verification, he nonchalantly dropped a bombshell: "I don't have pay stubs because I'm paid under the table." Well, isn't that convenient? But the real kicker came next. Tony, bless his adventurous spirit, boldly declared, "But I can pay you 6 months' rent in advance if you let me move in today."

Call me a skeptic, but when someone dangles a wad of cash in front of me like a carrot on a stick, my landlord senses start tingling. It's like a sixth sense honed from years of dealing with all sorts of characters. So, I paused for a moment, trying to process the audacity of this proposal. Who in their right mind would offer such a hefty sum upfront? Either this guy was a secret lottery winner or, more likely, he had something up his sleeve.

But, oh, dear reader, I took the bait in a moment of weakness and curiosity. I couldn't resist the allure of a financial windfall. I imagined the crisp dollar bills dancing in front of my eyes, taunting me with their promise of instant wealth. So, against my better judgment, I accepted Tony's application and welcomed him into my rental realm.

Fast forward six months, and it was time to face the music. The day of reckoning arrived, and Tony vanished into thin air like a mischievous genie. What he left behind, however, was far from magical. My once pristine unit resembled a disaster zone—a battleground of broken toilets, carpets adorned with doggy doodles, and wait for it, an empty garage with no door in sight. The audacity! The nerve! I was left scratching my head and muttering, "WTF just happened?"

Lesson learned, my friends. Trust me when I say that the allure of easy money is often a mirage in the desert of landlording. From that day forward, I made a vow to myself: I shall trust and verify. No more falling for sweet-talking tenants with outlandish offers. If it's not a resounding yes, backed up by concrete evidence and thorough vetting, it's a definite no. After all, sleepless nights and heart palpitations are not worth any amount of cash, no matter how enticing it may seem.

So, let Tony's tale serve as a reminder, a comical cautionary tale in the annals of landlording mishaps. And as I bid you farewell, my fellow landlords, always remember: trust your instincts, be wary of monetary mirages, and let laughter be your companion on this wild journey called landlording.

Chapter 8:
Embracing Healthy Vacancies

As a landlord, I've had my fair share of experiences in the rental market; let me tell you, it's a wild and unpredictable ride. One thing I've learned along the way is the importance of healthy vacancies and staying competitive. You might be thinking, "But why would I want vacancies? Isn't that bad for business?" Well, my fellow landlords, let me enlighten you.

Picture this: you have all your apartments rented out, and not a single unit is available. On the surface, it might seem like a great achievement, a testament to your landlord skills. But hold your horses because that might not be the case. Having no vacancies can be a sign that you're not charging market rates or missing out on potential growth opportunities. Yep, it's true!

You see, a healthy turnover rate is like the seasoning in your rental business recipe. It adds flavor and keeps things interesting. When tenants come and go, it indicates that your asking rent is aligned with the market rates. So, if you find yourself with a vacancy rate of around 5%, pat yourself on the back because that means you're doing something right.

Now, how do you ensure you're charging the right amount? It's time to become a market research ninja. Get your landlord cape on and embark on a quest to gather information about rental rates in your area. One tried-and-true method is reaching out to your competitors within a 2-mile radius. Give them a call, strike up a conversation, and ask about their rental prices. Trust me, it's like going undercover, except you're not a secret agent; you're just a curious landlord trying to stay in the game.

But wait, there's more! The digital realm is your playground. Platforms like Craigslist are treasure troves of rental listings. So, grab your laptop, a cup of coffee (or your beverage of choice), and start scrolling through the ads in your area. Take note of what other landlords are asking for similar properties. It's like window shopping, but you're scouting the rental market instead of checking out the latest fashion trends. Who knew being a landlord could be so fashionable?

Oh, and let's not forget the power of conversation. When prospective tenants view your property, seize the opportunity to engage with them. Strike up a conversation, make them feel at ease, and casually ask about the rental rates they've encountered during their apartment hunt. You'd be surprised how willing people are to spill the beans. It's like playing a "Who's Got the Best Deal?" game and gathering valuable intel along the way.

Armed with all this information, you can fine-tune your pricing strategy and ensure you're staying competitive. Remember, it's not just about charging the highest rent possible; it's about finding that sweet spot where tenants see the value in what you offer. It's like a delicate dance of balancing profit and attracting tenants. And let me tell you, it's a dance floor where landlords and tenants do the rent shuffle.

I know what you're thinking: "But what if my competitors have secret moves I don't know about?" Fear not, my landlord comrades! Knowledge is power, and by staying aware of your competitors and understanding the rental landscape, you position yourself as a formidable player in the game. You're like the Sherlock Holmes of the rental world, always one step ahead, solving the mystery of optimal rental pricing.

But remember, the rental market is a rollercoaster ride, and you need to hold on tight. Trends change, demands fluctuate, and you must adapt. So, don't just set it and forget it. Regularly review and reassess your rental rates, considering market dynamics, the demand in your area, and the value you provide to your tenants. It's like being a master chef, adjusting the seasoning to create the perfect dish that keeps your tenants returning for more.

Ultimately, embracing healthy vacancies and staying competitive is about finding the right balance between profit and tenant satisfaction. It's a journey of continuous learning, adaptation, and occasional laughter at the absurdity of it all. So, my fellow landlords, let's don our imaginary capes, embrace healthy vacancies like the rental market superheroes, and remember to sprinkle a dash of fun and humor along the way. Because hey, if you can't laugh in this wild world of rentals, what's the point?

Now go forth, my comrades, and may your vacancies be healthy, your rental rates be competitive, and your journey as a landlord be filled with personal growth, profitable returns, and the occasional chuckle.

Chapter 9:
How to Determine Asking Rent

"Why are you asking for such a high deposit?"

Ah, the age-old question of determining the perfect rent for my apartments. Pricing is a crucial consideration that can make or break the appeal of a rental property. As I navigate the complex world of property management, I've developed my own approach to setting rental rates—one that involves a bit of detective work and a dash of strategic thinking. So, grab a seat and join me on this amusing adventure as I unravel the mysteries of pricing in the rental market.

To begin my quest for the ideal rental rate, I turn to my trusty companion, Google. Armed with my laptop and a cup of coffee, I embark on a virtual journey through the vast realm of online listings. I search for comparable apartments within a three-mile radius of my properties. This search allows me to gauge the current market rate— the prevailing prices in the area.

But dear reader, I don't stop there. Oh no, I take it further by engaging in the lost art of conversation. I pick up the phone and call those competitors with enticing listings. It's like being an undercover agent, gathering vital intelligence in the battle for the best rental rates. Through these conversations, I discover their asking rates and absorb their wisdom, soaking up every tidbit of information.

Armed with this treasure trove of knowledge, I retreat to my lair and begin the delicate process of analysis. I calculate the average rates I've gathered from my covert phone calls. This becomes my reference point, the anchor that keeps me grounded in the reality of the market. But here's the secret sauce, my dear friends—I don't stop at the market rate. Oh no, I employ a cunning strategy to attract the best tenants and keep my vacancy rate low.

In my mischievous pursuit of desirable tenants, I offer a modest discount—around 5-7% below the market rate. Ah, the allure of a good deal! For most renters, every dollar counts, and by positioning myself slightly below the average, I capture their attention. But here's where the plot thickens—I ask for a higher security deposit, typically 1.5 times the monthly rent. Yes, you heard that right!

Now, you may be wondering why I would ask for more money upfront? Allow me to shed some light on this peculiar strategy. You see, dear reader, good tenants—the ones who take care of my property and treat it like their own—recognize the value of a well-maintained living space. They understand that their full security deposit will be returned to them when they eventually move out, provided they leave everything in good condition. So, by requesting a higher deposit, I attract tenants who appreciate the value of a well-kept home and provide myself with an additional layer of protection.

Ah, the comedy of rental pricing! While some landlords may be tempted to offer extravagant deals like "first three months free," I firmly believe such tactics are like a circus tightrope act—thrilling but ultimately destined for a fall. Let's consider the tenant who moves into a place rent-free for three months. Can we really expect them to suddenly conjure up the full rent on the fourth month? I think not! More often than not, this scenario leads to a troublesome cycle of searching for new tenants every few months—something I'd rather avoid.

So, my fellow adventurers in property management, I encourage you to strike a delicate balance in the art of pricing. Research your market, engage in conversation, and uncover the optimal rental rate for your properties. And remember, dear reader, that by offering a slight discount below the market rate while requesting a higher security deposit, you can attract quality tenants who appreciate the value of a well-maintained home. Together, let us embark on this hilarious journey of rental pricing, where strategy and wit prevail over circus-like antics.

Chapter 10:
The Curse of the Unfinished Unit

"Should I start marketing the unit even though it's not 100% ready?"

As I delve deeper into the world of property management, a question often haunts my mind: "Should I start pre-marketing this unit now?" Oh, the temptation to get ahead of the game can be overpowering. But fear not, my friends, for within this essay, I shall unravel the mysteries of perfect timing. Get ready to discover the art of unit preparation and why advertising should only begin when your unit is 100% ready for its grand debut.

Imagine this scenario, if you will: I am a landlord eagerly searching for the perfect tenant. Pre-leasing or pre-advertising an unfinished unit crosses my mind. Oh, the allure of enticing potential tenants before the unit is truly ready! But let me be crystal clear, my dear readers: treading this path is treacherous, leading only to wasted time and unnecessary stress.

In the kingdom of landlording, a cardinal rule reigns supreme: never start advertising until the unit is 100% prepared for showing. This means it must be impeccably clean, repairs completed, and every aspect in order. Pre-leasing or pre-advertising is nothing more than a mirage, a false hope that ensnares landlords in a trap.

Now, you may wonder, why is pre-marketing such a futile endeavor? The answer lies in the quality of potential tenants. Envision those who would consider an unfinished unit—desperation lurks in their shadows. They may be individuals facing homelessness or those who have been evicted from their previous dwellings. Either way, their circumstances lead them to settle for less-than-ideal living conditions. And as a landlord, trust me when I say these are the tenants you want to avoid.

Now, let's take a lighthearted detour into the whimsical dance of the unfinished unit. Imagine yourself as a participant in this amusing spectacle. On one side of the ballroom, there's an eager landlord, yearning to find a tenant. On the other side, potential tenants, longing for a place to call home. The music begins, and the landlord, unable to resist the temptation, starts pre-marketing an unfinished unit. But alas, the dance is fraught with missteps and stumbles. The potential tenants, cautious of the incomplete offering, pirouette away, leaving the landlord in a state of frustration and regret.

In the realm of successful property management, timing reigns supreme. The art of unit preparation teaches us the value of patience, the importance of resisting the allure of pre-marketing, and the necessity of waiting until our units are 100% ready for their grand unveiling. Let us not be swayed by the illusion of pre-leasing or pre-advertising, for it is a path that leads to stress and undesirable tenants. Instead, my fellow readers, let us bide our time, ensuring every part of the unit is impeccable. And then, and only then, shall we release the siren call of our marketing efforts.

To conclude, my friends, remember that a successful property management journey requires mastering the art of perfect timing. Resist the temptation to jump the gun, patiently prepare your unit until it shines, and watch as the right tenants flock to your doorstep. Let us bid farewell to the treacherous path of pre-marketing and embrace the realm of impeccable unit preparation. In this realm, dear readers, lies the key to finding not just any tenant but the perfect tenant for your rental property.

Chapter 11:
The Quest for the Elusive Rent Payment

"No, we do not take cash!"

Welcome to the exhilarating roller coaster ride of rent collection! This tale is filled with triumphs, mishaps, and uproarious misadventures that unfold when cash takes center stage. Join me as we explore the whimsical and often chaotic world of landlords desperately chasing tenants for rent payments, only to discover a better, more efficient way to handle this monetary dance. Prepare to embark on a laughter-filled journey as we dive into the chapter "No, We Don't Take Cash!"

In the early days of my career as a landlord, I found myself entangled in a peculiar predicament. With a portfolio of 110 units, I took it upon myself to personally collect rent from each tenant. Oh, the innocence of my actions! Little did I know the comedic chaos that awaited me.

As the first day of the month arrived, I would set off on a whimsical adventure, knocking on doors hoping to retrieve rent payments from my tenants. But alas, the universe had a different plan in store for me. Half of the time, I would encounter empty homes or unanswered doors—a silent reminder that the rent was nowhere to be found.

What followed was a spectacle of persistence and absurdity. Day after day, I would return to the properties, chasing down tenants in pursuit of the elusive rent. I even ventured into the dimly lit corners of scrappy and dangerous neighborhoods, braving the unknown, all searching for the almighty dollar.

And when those tenants who couldn't fulfill their obligations finally opened their doors, a symphony of excuses filled the air. Stories of dogs devouring rent money, bosses failing to pay on time, and wallets mysteriously vanishing would grace my ears. This exhausting dance played out month after month, leaving me feeling like a desperate beggar, pleading for what was rightfully mine.

Let's take a moment to imagine a bustling circus tent—a vibrant world where landlords and tenants come together in a spectacle of laughter and absurdity. In one corner, a landlord juggles rent payment demands, while tenants perform a balancing act of creative excuses in the other. The ringmaster, torn between frustration and amusement, desperately tries to maintain order. Welcome to the Cash Collection Circus, where reality bends, and laughter reigns supreme.

Reflecting on those uproarious and chaotic days, a revelation struck me like a lightning bolt. Why, oh why, was I relentlessly chasing after tenants for my hard-earned money? It was time to turn the tables on this cash collection comedy, to flip the script. And so I devised a plan to bring order and efficiency to rent payments.

With newfound determination, I issued notices to all tenants, announcing a change in protocol. I instructed them to set up Zelle or bank transfers and make sure their rent reached my account by 5 PM on the first day of the month. Failure to comply would result in a hefty $100 fee, including late fees and notice charges. No exceptions. It was time for the stick to take center stage, for people to realize the importance of fulfilling their obligations when their pockets were at stake.

In this grand comedic tale, we learn that people are more inclined to listen when it directly affects their wallets. The carrot may be tempting, but the stick truly grabs attention. The balance of power shifted by making tenants responsible for delivering their rent, and chaos transformed into order.

Since starting the revolutionary "Zelle-Only Rent Collection System," my life as a landlord has taken an extraordinary turn. Gone are the days of awkward knocking on doors and pleading for rent.

Like magic, I wake up on the 1st of every month to a flood of Zelle transfers—a symphony of chimes on my phone that sings, "Rent, rent, glorious rent!"

Excuses like, "The bank is closed on Sundays, sorry!" are no longer part of my vocabulary. Oh no, my friends, the power of Zelle knows no bounds! Now, my tenants can effortlessly zap their rent to me with a simple swipe on their phones. It's like a rent-paying revolution, and I am the mighty Zelle Wizard, seeing the flow of money into my bank account with sheer delight.

But that's not all! My bank statement has become a treasure map, revealing the names of all the brave souls who dared to transfer their hard-earned cash. I no longer have to endure the headaches of tracking elusive tenants and playing hide-and-seek with rent money. Now, I stroll through my statement, waving at the names of responsible payers and letting out a mischievous chuckle at those who try to escape my watchful eye.

And the best part? It saves me a whopping ten hours every month! Ten glorious hours I can dedicate to other landlord pursuits, like scheming deviously or perfecting my "Rent Collection Dance." Who could have guessed that a simple app could grant me such freedom and joy?

So, fellow landlords, join me in embracing the Zelle revolution! Bid farewell to door-knocking and rent-chasing, and let the magical realm of mobile transfers guide us toward a brighter, rent-filled future!

Chapter 12:
The Rules, the Exceptions, and the Unyielding Landlord

"No, You Need to Follow the Rules, No Exceptions!"

In the early days of my rental career, I proudly wore the badge of the "nice guy." I genuinely believed in giving my tenants second chances and bending the rules in the name of compassion. However, as the saying goes, "No good deed goes unpunished," and I soon found myself caught in a web of my own creation.

One area where my kindness often backfired was in the realm of fees. Late fees and notice fees were intended to serve as deterrents, ensuring tenants paid their rent on time. But as the self-proclaimed "nice guy," I often succumbed to my tenants' pleas, waiving the fees in exchange for promises of timely payments in the future.

Once upon a time, in the whimsical land of Landlordia, I made the fateful mistake of caving into my tenants' outlandish excuses for not paying rent on time. Little did I know this seemingly innocent decision would set off a chain reaction of comedic chaos! In my benevolent quest to be the nice guy, I bent my rules and forgave the late fees. Alas, the consequences were far from pleasant. Unbeknownst to me, I unwittingly became the laughingstock of Landlordia. My tenants discovered that my rules and words were as flimsy as a feather in a hurricane. They realized the ultimate superpower: talking themselves out of any responsibility! And so, a symphony of late rental payments reverberated through the once-peaceful halls of my abode. It was a spectacle of absurdity, worthy of a place in the comedic hall of fame. Who could have predicted that my well-intentioned act of kindness would unleash a wave of tardiness like no other? It was a lesson learned the hard way—that being a nice guy can sometimes lead to the most ludicrous of outcomes!

Reflecting on those comical and challenging moments, a revelation struck me like a bolt of lightning—I had become the enabler of my misfortune. By waiving fees and bending the rules, I unintentionally opened the floodgates for tenants to take advantage of my kindness. It was time for a change, a shift in mindset and approach.

This uproarious chapter reveals the vital importance of upholding rules without exceptions. By adopting a firm stance and charging fees without leniency, tenants will understand that the rules are non-negotiable. No longer will my generosity be mistaken for weakness. The mantra became clear: "No, you need to follow the rules, no exceptions."

So, fellow landlords, let us bid farewell to the pitfalls of being the "nice guy." From this moment forward, we shall stand strong, unwavering in our commitment to the rules that govern our landlord-tenant relationships. Join me in the upcoming chapters, where we shall navigate the labyrinth of tenant disputes, unravel the mysteries of property maintenance, and discover the secrets to a harmonious and profitable landlording journey. Remember, dear readers, in the firmness of our resolve we safeguard our investments and thrive as successful landlords.

Chapter 13:
Tales of the Rent Excuse Chronicles

"Dog Ate My Rent Money!"

In the vast tapestry of landlording, one must always be ready to encounter an array of excuses from tenants when it comes to paying rent on time. As the gatekeeper of our livelihood, it is imperative to establish and uphold a set of rules that leaves no room for flexibility. In this chapter, I invite you to explore the tenants' repertoire of stories and discover the unyielding landlord's approach to handling these tales.

Regarding rent collection in today's world, my rule of thumb is simple—no excuses, no exceptions. Tenants may come forth with tearful stories of lost jobs, sick relatives, or even the infamous "dog ate my rent money" scenario. However, as compassionate as we may be, we must remember that our role as landlords is not that of private investigators or charity workers. Our primary responsibility is to maintain the financial stability of our properties and ensure that rent is paid on time.

Now, let's take a lighthearted detour into the realm of excuses with a humorous interlude. Picture a landlord caught in the whirlwind of sympathy, waiving fees for a tenant who claimed his father's passing as the reason for late rent. Months later, the same tenant reemerges with an identical tale, only to backtrack and claim his mother had passed away. Now feeling foolish, the landlord realizes the dangers of falling into the trap of excuses and the downward spiral that awaits when leniency prevails.

Our role in landlording is that of shrewd businesspeople, not benevolent charity workers. While it is admirable to contribute to charitable causes outside of our business endeavors, it is essential to draw a clear line regarding rent collection. By adhering to a strict set of rules and disregarding the creative tales tenants may spin, we protect our investments and maintain the stability of our livelihoods.

We must remember that while compassion is a virtue, it must be channeled appropriately. As landlords, we uphold the agreement between tenant and landlord—a safe and comfortable home in exchange for timely rent payments. By treating our rental properties as businesses rather than charities, we create an environment of professionalism and respect.

So, my fellow landlords, let us bid farewell to the convoluted world of rent excuses and embrace the unyielding spirit within us. Join me in the upcoming chapters, where we shall uncover the secrets of property maintenance, unravel the complexities of landlord-tenant relationships, and navigate the ever-changing landscape of the landlording industry. Remember, dear readers, in the realm of rent excuses, our steadfastness shall prevail, protecting our investments and ensuring our success as unwavering landlords.

Chapter 14:
The Eviction Chronicles

"All rise for the eviction hearing."

Welcome, dear readers, to a chapter exploring the thrilling eviction world. Buckle up as we delve into reclaiming your property from non-paying tenants. Join us as we navigate the intricacies of eviction court, encounters with creative excuses, and the costly aftermath of the eviction process. Get ready for a rollercoaster ride through the chapter "All Rise for the Eviction Hearing!"

In this chapter, we embark on a journey through eviction, from when rent is late to the day of reckoning in eviction court. Brace yourselves as we unravel the intricacies of serving notices, engaging with tenants, and facing the inevitable court battles.

Picture this, a tenant, caught in the web of eviction proceedings, vehemently denying ever receiving the crucial notice of upcoming eviction. To combat such claims, it is vital to adopt a multi-pronged approach. Hand-delivering the notice and taping it to their door, coupled with certified mail and proof of mailing, becomes essential evidence when facing eviction court. When it comes to the law, it is all about documentation and irrefutable proof.

Humorous Interlude: The Ridiculous Excuses

Ah, the tales we hear in the realm of evictions! From plumbing grievances to the mysterious realm of "invisible service requests," tenants never stop amazing us with their outrageous justifications for not paying rent. But fear not, dear readers, for we live in a state with conservative judges who see through the smoke and mirrors. As they repetitively ask, "Did you pay rent on time?" the tenants' convoluted excuses crumble under the weight of truth, leading to a favorable judgment for the diligent landlord.

While the triumph of winning an eviction case may bring a sense of relief, the aftermath is not without its challenges. The costs begin to add up as the tenants are given a grace period to vacate the premises. Repairing damages left behind, the loss of one month's rent, court fees, and the additional expenses incurred during the eviction process all contribute to a substantial financial setback for the landlord. The numbers quickly escalate, leaving one to ponder the importance of due diligence in selecting reliable tenants.

Alternative Solutions: Cash for Keys

To avoid the arduous and costly eviction process, wise landlords seek alternative solutions. Enter the idea of "cash for keys," where negotiations take place to incentivize tenants to vacate voluntarily. Landlords can save themselves from the time-consuming and expensive eviction process by offering financial compensation or returning a portion of their deposit. The choice becomes clear for the tenant: accept the offer and avoid eviction or face legal proceedings and a tarnished record.

Evictions are not to be taken lightly, as they bring forth significant financial burdens and time-consuming court battles. By emphasizing the importance of thorough tenant screening and conducting due diligence, landlords can prevent themselves from falling into the quagmire of eviction proceedings. Remember, dear readers, the key lies in foresight and preparation to ensure a smooth and prosperous landlording journey.

Chapter 15:
People Don't Change... Or Do They?

Let's delve into the intriguing world of tenant behavior and explore whether transformation is possible. Brace yourselves for a journey filled with humorous anecdotes, surprises, and the ultimate question: Can people change? Prepare to unravel the chapter "People Don't Change... Or Do They?"

As landlords, we often encounter troublemaker tenants who consistently disrupt the peace with loud music or perpetually pay their rent late. Conventional wisdom dictates these habits are deeply ingrained and unchangeable. But is that always the case?

As staunch believers in the theory that people don't change, we often lack empathy for tenants who consistently engage in problematic behavior. We view their actions as a permanent part of their identity, leaving no room for understanding or compassion. However, it is crucial to consider the repercussions of this mindset. We inadvertently create a self-fulfilling prophecy by closing ourselves off to the possibility of change. We deny ourselves the opportunity to address the root causes of their behavior and seek a resolution.

There comes a time when dealing with troublesome tenants becomes overwhelming. The stress and worry seep into every part of our lives, even when we're thousands of miles away on a well-deserved vacation. During these moments of realization, we must confront the situation head-on. The long-term benefits of peace of mind far outweigh the temporary discomfort we may experience while removing a bad tenant.

Humorous Interlude: The Chronicles of Vacation Woes

Imagine lounging on a tropical beach, margarita in hand, only to be bombarded with incessant phone calls and emails from tenants causing trouble. The serenity of vacation shatters, replaced by the chaos of tenant dramas. In these moments, we understand the importance of dealing with problem tenants promptly. As we sip our margaritas, we vow to take decisive action to safeguard our peace of mind, even if it means enduring short-term discomfort.

There is a balancing act every landlord should consider. Trading short-term pain for long-term gain! With newfound determination, we embark on ridding ourselves of problematic tenants. We recognize that it may involve short-term pain, such as eviction proceedings or searching for new tenants. However, we remain steadfast in believing that the long-term gain far outweighs the temporary inconvenience. By releasing ourselves from the burdens of problematic tenants, we open the door to a world of possibilities and a more peaceful landlord experience.

As we conclude this thought-provoking chapter, we question the validity of the belief that people are incapable of change. Although some individuals may resist transformation, it is essential to approach each tenant with an open mind and a willingness to seek resolution. By fostering empathy and addressing concerns head-on, we may be surprised by the potential for growth and positive change.

Chapter 16:
The Price of Precious Decimal Rent Amounts

"You need to pay your rent in exact amount!"

In this chapter, we will explore the meticulous system used by landlords to track rent payments with precision. Discover the reasoning behind this unique approach and the unexpected challenges that may arise.

Landlords like us employ a system where each unit's rent amount is tailored to create a unique figure. Using this method, we can easily identify who has paid and who hasn't. Let's examine the motivation behind this meticulous approach and its impact on our landlord experience.

The Quest for Clarity: Bank Account Balance on the 1st

Imagine waking up on the 1st of the month and eagerly checking your bank account to see which tenants have dutifully paid their rent. As I scroll through the transactions, the exactness of the decimal rent amounts allows for swift identification. The rent for Unit 18 is $1018.18, and the rent for Unit 55 is $1055.55. With a glance, I can assess the state of my rental income. In this pursuit of clarity and ease, the decimal rent system finds its purpose.

Let us explore the hilarious predicament when tenants fall short by a mere five cents. Picture this, you diligently monitor your bank account, only to discover that one tenant has underpaid their rent by a minuscule amount. They owe $1018.13 instead of the required $1018.18. A wave of amusement washes over you as you grapple with handling this penny-pinching conundrum. Do you ask the tenant for the measly sum or let it slide? Such scenarios serve as a reminder that the pursuit of exactness can sometimes lead to unexpected and humorous situations.

The underlying motivation for employing decimal rent amounts is rooted in a desire for efficiency and simplicity. As landlords, we strive to minimize the time and effort spent managing our rental properties, allowing us to enjoy the freedom of being 3000 miles away on vacation. By implementing a system that streamlines rent tracking, we create an environment that promotes peace of mind and maximizes our time for personal pursuits.

As we conclude this chapter, we reflect on the pros and cons of requesting rent payments with decimal precision. While the system provides a quick and easy method for identifying paid and unpaid tenants, it also presents humorous and unexpected challenges. As landlords, we must strike a balance between efficiency and flexibility, understanding that occasional discrepancies of a few cents should not overshadow the overall success of our landlord journey.

Chapter 17:
The Balancing Act of Rent Increases

"Your rent is going up next month!"

In this chapter, we delve into the importance of periodically adjusting the asking rent for existing tenants. Landlords like us understand the necessity of keeping up with rising costs and inflationary pressures. Join us as we explore the delicate balance between maintaining a profitable rental business and addressing the needs of our tenants.

The Financial Reality is that we have rising costs and inflation. As responsible business owners, we must face the reality that our expenses increase over time. From contractor costs and supplies for repairs to insurance premiums and utilities, the financial landscape constantly evolves. To ensure the continued viability of our rental properties, it becomes imperative to adjust rent to accommodate these rising costs. After all, no one wants to run a business that operates at a loss.

Psychological Preparedness: Setting Expectations

Beyond the financial aspect, keeping our tenants informed about the inevitable reality of rent increases due to inflation is crucial. By establishing regular rent adjustments, we create a psychological framework wherein tenants understand that periodic increases are part of the rental landscape. This transparency helps manage expectations and reduces surprises when rent adjustments occur.

The Pitfalls of Favoritism: A Lesson Learned

In our journey as landlords, we occasionally encounter situations where compassion tempts us to extend favors to long-term tenants. We might hesitate to increase rent for someone on a fixed income or facing financial difficulties. However, as the saying goes, "No good deed goes unpunished." We must be mindful of the consequences that can arise from playing favorites. A prime example is the retired tenant whose rent remained unchanged for over four years. When the time finally came to adjust her rent by a mere 5%, she reacted with anger and accusations of discrimination. This serves as a stark reminder that it is in our best interest, as well as the tenant's, to adhere to a fair and consistent rent increase policy.

Conclusion:

Annual rent increase is a delicate matter. It is a balancing act between financial responsibility and tenant relations. By acknowledging the rising costs of running a rental property business and setting realistic expectations for rent adjustments, we can navigate this process more easily. Remember, dear readers, that effective communication and consistency are key when implementing rent increases.

Chapter 18:
Lessons Learned - Fool Me Once

This chapter is dedicated to the valuable lessons we've learned as landlords. In this chapter titled "Fool Me Once," we delve into the importance of sticking to our principles and following our established rules. Join us as we explore the consequences of bending our guidelines and the wisdom gained from past experiences.

We confront the reality of dealing with tenants who consistently fail to meet their rental obligations. As landlords, we may be tempted to make agreements and give second chances, hoping tenants will fulfill their promises. However, we soon discover that such efforts are often in vain. Join us as we explore the importance of sticking to our principles and avoiding unnecessary headaches.

We've all experienced situations where tenants promise to pay their rent and associated fees if given more time. Unfortunately, more often than not, these promises are empty and go unfulfilled. We must acknowledge that once a tenant breaks an agreement and becomes unresponsive, it is time to take immediate action. Their words lose meaning, and we must prioritize our well-being and financial stability.

Our rules and guidelines exist for a reason. Through trial and error, we have paid the "tuition" necessary to learn valuable lessons in dealing with troublesome tenants. It is essential to adhere to these rules and regulations to save ourselves from unnecessary headaches and additional work. By doing so, we maintain consistency and avoid the pitfalls of deviating from our established principles.

In landlord-tenant relationships, it is vital to remember that this is a business, and our primary responsibility is to protect our interests. We must prioritize our financial stability and adhere to the necessary protocols outlined by law. By doing what we are supposed to do, right at this very moment, we maintain a sense of professionalism and ensure that our business remains intact.

The repercussions can be severe when we veer from our rules and guidelines. Providing fewer warnings or notices to delinquent tenants may initially seem like a cost-saving measure. Still, it only increases headaches and additional work in the long run. By ignoring our own established protocols, we invite chaos and make our jobs more challenging.

It is crucial to stay true to our principles, follow our established rules, and prioritize our well-being in dealing with troublesome tenants. By recognizing that empty promises and bending the rules only lead to more headaches, we can navigate the challenges of property management with wisdom and foresight.

Chapter 19:
Breaking My Own Rules

This chapter explores the dangers of deviating from our established principles and the consequences of breaking our own rules. Join us as we learn valuable lessons from real-life experiences and discover the importance of maintaining a firm and consistent approach in property management.

Now let's discuss the Slippery Slope of Waiving Fees. As a landlord, it is tempting to be understanding and lenient with tenants facing hardships. However, we must remember that rules are in place for a reason. In this chapter, we delve into the pitfalls of breaking our own rules and the consequences that follow.

Waiving fees for tenants who fail to pay rent on time may seem like an act of kindness, but it can quickly turn into a slippery slope. By doing so, we unintentionally become "enablers" of bad behavior. Tenants may take advantage of our leniency, pushing the boundaries and repeatedly expecting special treatment.

In life, we often hear the saying, "You can catch more flies with honey than with vinegar." However, in the world of property management, the opposite holds true. Tenants are more likely to respond to the stick rather than the carrot. By enforcing strict rules and consequences, we set clear expectations and establish a sense of accountability.

Instead of rewarding bad behavior by waiving fees, we should focus on providing incentives for good behavior. For example, offering a small discount on rent for tenants who consistently pay on time can motivate them to meet their obligations promptly. Positive reinforcement encourages tenants to uphold their end of the agreement.

I firmly believe in the principle of "Smile but Stay Firm" When dealing with tenants, it's essential to maintain a pleasant and approachable demeanor. A warm smile can go a long way in building rapport. However, it is equally crucial to remain firm and assertive in upholding the rules and policies of the rental agreement. By striking this balance, we create a professional environment that commands respect.

Tenants who sense leniency may continuously test the limits to see how far they can push before facing the consequences. By adhering strictly to our rules and not bending them, we demonstrate that there is no room for negotiation when meeting their obligations.

A real-life example, like that of tenant Alfonso, illustrates the potential consequences of breaking our rules. In an act of goodwill, I gave him extra time to pay rent and waived fees. Sadly, he exploited my kindness. He promised to pay the full amount plus the late fees by the middle of them month. But instead, he just moved out, leaving me a damaged apartment and lived there free for half a month. This unfortunate outcome highlights the importance of adhering to strict policies.

I cannot emphasize enough the importance of sticking to our principles and avoiding the pitfalls of breaking our own rules. Maintaining a firm and consistent property management approach fosters a sense of accountability and respect among our tenants. Let us learn from the lessons shared in this chapter and continue to navigate the world of rental property management with wisdom and unwavering resolve.

Chapter 20:
The Eviction Chronicles II -
Beware of the Professional
Evictees

This chapter delves into the world of "professional evictees". We learn from real-life experiences and gain insights into navigating these challenging situations with caution and wisdom.

As landlords, we encounter various types of tenants, but one group that requires extra vigilance is the "professional evictees." These individuals have a history of frequent evictions and have become well-versed in the legal nuances and loopholes of the eviction process. They know how to manipulate the system to extend their stay rent-free.

In our desire to work with struggling tenants, we may be tempted to accept partial rent payments or payment arrangements. However, this can be a trap that professional evictors exploit. Accepting partial payments prolongs the eviction process and weakens our case if we end up in court.

An example from my own experience involved a tenant named Victoria. We agreed on a payment arrangement where she would pay half the rent on the 5th and the remaining half plus late fees on the 20th. Unfortunately, Victoria broke her promise and failed to make the second payment. I faced an unexpected setback in court when I initiated the eviction process.

In Victoria's case, the judge ruled that I had to return the first partial payment before proceeding with the eviction. This ruling left me in a frustrating position, as it meant starting the eviction process all over again while Victoria continued to reside in my property without paying rent. It was a hard lesson learned, highlighting the importance of avoiding partial payments altogether.

Professional evictees like Victoria have perfected their strategies over time. Once aware of their history, it is crucial to exercise extreme caution. Providing a second chance to tenants with a track record of evictions is not worth the risk. Their repeated encounters with the eviction process clearly indicate their disregard for moral and financial responsibilities.

Going to court for eviction is always a gamble. The outcome can be unpredictable, and a judgment against us can lead to further delays and frustrations. By learning from experiences like Victoria's case, we become better equipped to navigate eviction and protect ourselves from professional evictees.

This chapter has shed light on the existence of professional evictees and the dangers associated with accepting partial rent payments. By understanding their tactics and learning from real-life experiences, we can take necessary precautions to safeguard our properties and minimize the risk of prolonged and costly evictions. Moving forward, let us remain vigilant, avoid second chances for tenants with eviction histories, and continue to manage our rental properties with prudence and wisdom.

Chapter 21:
The Power of Silence -
Lessons Learned from Eviction
Proceedings

"Over prepare and listen in silence."

This chapter explores the valuable lessons gained from the numerous eviction proceedings I have encountered throughout my landlord career. We discover the power of silence, the art of listening, and the importance of careful preparation when dealing with tenant disputes in court.

Experience has taught me the importance of thorough preparation before entering an eviction proceeding. By familiarizing myself with the case details, gathering evidence, and understanding the legal requirements, I am better equipped to present my side effectively. However, one of the most valuable skills I have learned is the art of listening.

During an eviction hearing, while it can be tempting to argue and assert our position during the proceedings, silence can be a powerful tool. By keeping my mouth shut and allowing the defendant or tenant to speak, I have witnessed how they often talk themselves into losing the case. People tend to reveal crucial information or make damaging statements when given the opportunity. Silence gives them room to expose their weaknesses.

In eviction court, I have found that less is often more. By listening attentively and allowing the tenant to present their case, I gain valuable insights into their arguments, which can ultimately work in my favor. The more they talk, the more opportunities they provide for their case to weaken.

Court proceedings are inherently unpredictable, and the outcome can depend on various factors. To mitigate risks, I have learned to handle tenant issues before they reach court. Addressing concerns such as pest infestations or repairs in a timely manner helps resolve disputes and strengthens my position in court, should the need arise.

In today's digital age, text messages can serve as valuable evidence. To protect myself and strengthen my case, I make it a practice to request and retain text confirmations of important discussions or agreements with tenants. These records provide a clear and documented communication trail, leaving little room for misinterpretation or false claims.

In conclusion, this chapter has shed light on the power of silence and the art of listening in eviction proceedings. We increase our chances of a favorable outcome by over-preparing, remaining silent, and allowing tenants to speak their minds. Court can be unpredictable, but we position ourselves for success by addressing tenant issues proactively and utilizing text confirmations as evidence. As we continue our journey as landlords, let us remember the power of silence and the importance of careful preparation when facing tenant disputes in court.

Chapter 22:
The Mysterious Case of the Vanishing Tenant

"What? Who died?"

In this chapter, we delve into the perplexing story of Jerry, the bedridden tenant who mysteriously passed away without my knowledge. Join me as we navigate the absurdities and frustrations that ensued when dealing with government agencies and the surprising financial consequences that followed.

Jerry, an 80-year-old bedridden tenant, resided with her extended family in one of my three-bedroom units. She received monthly government assistance, Section 8, to cover her rent. Little did I know that Jerry's life and her tenancy were about to take an unexpected turn.

During the global COVID-19 pandemic, tragedy struck when Jerry passed away in a local hospital. Astonishingly, her family neglected to inform me or the agency responsible for her rental benefits about her untimely demise. Unaware of her passing, I continued to receive rent payments from the government agency as if everything was normal.

Six months later, Jerry's family decided to move out of the unit. At this point, the agency responsible for her rental benefits discovered her passing, which had occurred half a year earlier. Shockingly, they demanded that I return six months' rent, totaling a staggering $8,500. I found myself caught in the middle of a baffling situation.

Here is where the blame game begins. Despite not knowing of Jerry's passing or the events transpiring within her household, the agency insisted that I should have been aware. They argued that since she was their client, I was responsible for monitoring her situation. However, as a landlord, I had no reason to inspect her unit, especially since they were supposedly good tenants who caused no trouble.

Seeking justice, I contacted the federal agency in charge of rental benefits, hoping they would understand the absurdity of the situation and rectify the error. To my dismay, they shrugged off my concerns and deducted the $8,500 from their monthly payments without allowing me to appeal their decision. It felt like I was battling against an impenetrable bureaucracy.

The experience disillusioned me with government agencies and their unilateral decision-making powers. It became abundantly clear that dealing with them was daunting, as they could make arbitrary decisions, even when they were wrong. From that moment forward, I adopted extra caution and diligence when interacting with government entities.

Here, we've witnessed the absurdity of Jerry's passing and the subsequent financial predicament it caused. The story serves as a cautionary tale about the unpredictability of government agencies and the challenges landlords face when navigating their complex systems. As we continue our journey through the rental property world, remember the importance of thorough documentation, open communication, and a healthy dose of skepticism when dealing with governmental entities.

This chapter has taken us on a wild ride through the mysterious case of Jerry, a tenant who vanished from my property due to an unfortunate demise. We've witnessed the frustrating aftermath of her passing, the unexpected financial burden placed upon me, and the indifference of government agencies. This story serves as a reminder to remain vigilant, exercise caution, and be prepared for the unexpected when dealing with bureaucratic systems. In the following chapters, we will explore additional tales, share more lessons learned, and continue our quest for successful property management amidst the unpredictable nature of the rental world.

Chapter 23:
When Ignorance Sparks a Neighborhood High

"Zero tolerance for drugs."

In this chapter, we dive into the unexpected consequences that unfolded when I turned a blind eye to a potential drug-dealing situation. Join me as we explore the hilarious and eye-opening journey that ensued, teaching me valuable lessons about honesty, responsibility, and the importance of addressing red flags head-on.

Our story begins with a tenant who seemed like a model resident—a military veteran living on disability and military benefits. With a knee problem from his time in the military, he kept his front porch spotless and even took it upon himself to maintain the cleanliness of the parking lot using his trusty blower. It was a seemingly perfect arrangement, as he contributed his services free of charge, driven by his desire for a tidy environment.

Three years into his tenancy, a cloud of suspicion began to form around my unsuspecting tenant. Rumors started circulating among his neighbors that he might be involved in drug dealing, even though he claimed it was for medicinal purposes due to his doctor-prescribed marijuana usage. Initially, I took his explanation at face value, thinking he had a legitimate reason for using marijuana to alleviate his knee pain. Oh, how wrong I was!

When confronted with the unsettling rumors, I found myself at a crossroads. Should I kick him out immediately or simply issue a warning? I thought he was harmless and helpful, so I looked the other way. Little did I know that this choice would set off a chain reaction of chaos and disruption within my once-peaceful complex.

Soon after, my complex morphed into a haven for all manner of druggies seeking their next fix. The atmosphere grew increasingly tense, prompting three of my existing tenants to flee the scene, seeking solace elsewhere. As vacancies multiplied, the abandoned units became prime targets for break-ins by the very individuals my inaction had unwittingly attracted.

As I pen these words, it has been six long months since the eviction process began. The aftermath of my ill-conceived decision still looms large, draining my coffers and leaving me with a sinking feeling of regret. The losses in revenue due to the vacant units have stacked up, serving as a painful reminder of the price I paid for my oversight.

This cautionary tale has taught me some invaluable life lessons. I now realize the importance of acting responsibly, taking the time to investigate when red flags emerge, and never disregarding potential illegal activities. Trusting my instincts and addressing concerns promptly is paramount to maintaining a safe and harmonious living environment for all tenants.

This chapter has shed light on the disastrous consequences that unfolded when I ignored warning signs and tolerated illegal activities within my rental property. Through this humbling experience, I've learned the importance of integrity, honesty, and always adhering to the law. Remember, when in doubt, choose the path of legality and never underestimate the power of due diligence.

Chapter 24:
A Lesson in Sublet Shenanigans

"Please let me do this; I'll pay you!"

In this chapter, we will discuss Hunter, a tenant with a not-so-clever subletting scheme. Get ready to laugh, gasp, and learn the true value of integrity and peace of mind in the unpredictable world of landlordship.

Our tale begins with Hunter, a tenant whose rent was being covered by a government agency. Seeking to boost her bank account, she hatched a plan to sublet her unit to a friend while offering me an under-the-table bribe. Oh, the audacity! Little did Hunter know, she was about to stumble into a whirlwind of comedic misfortune.

When faced with Hunter's outrageous proposition, I couldn't help but burst into laughter. Did she think I'd risk my integrity for a few extra bucks? Oh, the comedic genius of the situation! With a twinkle in my eye, I quickly decided to report Hunter's shenanigans to the government agency, much to her dismay.

As the agency caught wind of Hunter's ill-conceived subletting scheme, they wasted no time in booting her from their program. Cue the dramatic exit! Oh, the irony of it all. While I bid farewell to the steady stream of rent, I relished the priceless satisfaction of knowing I had outwitted a not-so-clever con artist.

In a world of slippery slopes and dubious deals, I found solace in the uproarious power of integrity. Who needs a secret stash of cash when you can have the genuine satisfaction of doing the right thing? Oh, the bellyaching laughter ensued as I revealed my decision to prioritize honesty over Hunter's harebrained scheme.

As I basked in the joyous glow of my choice, the true hilarity unfolded. My dear readers, peace of mind is a precious gem worth more than all the under-the-table payments in the world. With each passing day, I chuckled at the absurdity of Hunter's failed plot and relished the tranquility of knowing I had chosen the high road.

This tale of subletting shenanigans serves as a reminder that laughter and integrity can go hand in hand. By thwarting Hunter's not-so-cunning plan, I protected my business and contributed to the collective chuckles of the rental industry. Oh, the comedy gold that comes from upholding our principles and showing those scheming tenants the door!

This chapter has regaled us with the sidesplitting chronicles of Hunter's subletting fiasco and the subsequent triumph of integrity and peace of mind. As we navigate the unpredictable landscape of landlordship, let us never forget the priceless comedy that ensues when we choose honesty over deception.

Chapter 25:
The Late Rent Chronicles - From Enabler to Enforcer

"I am sorry, but I have to pay rent late again this month!"

Our story begins with a recurring character, the tenant who consistently pays rent late, month after month. Oh, the comedy of repeating patterns! It's time to end this madness, as I finally realize that my enabling ways have only led to being pushed around. Cue the laughter, my friends, for the tide is about to turn!

Claudio's Comedy of Fees

First on the stage is Claudio, a tenant who always tested the boundaries of late payments. Determined to break free from the cycle, I mustered the courage to enforce my rules. With standard fees plus an additional $10 daily, Claudio's world was turned upside down. Oh, the hilarity that ensued as he swiftly packed his bags and bid adieu to my property. A vacancy filled, and a headache avoided. Victory!

Anthony's Late Nightmares

Next up, we have Anthony, the hardworking single dad juggling multiple jobs to support his adorable brood of three little rascals. Oh, the sympathy that tugged at my heartstrings! I let my emotions cloud my judgment and permitted him to be late for six consecutive months. What a mistake! The punchline? Anthony had the audacity to claim that his tardy rent payments had become the new norm and that I had no right to suddenly enforce late fees. The gall of this guy! Lesson learned: No favors for anyone. It's time to rid myself of non-paying tenants and embrace the mantra that vacancies will be filled without worry if the price is right.

Crystal's Promises and Lies

Last but not least, we encounter Crystal, the master of deception and broken promises. Oh, the foolishness of enabling her behavior! Instead of swiftly filing for eviction at the first sign of broken trust, I was entangled in a frustrating web of lies. Cue the laughter, my dear readers, as I realized that babysitting and parenting tenants were not in my job description. Lesson learned: No more frustration, no more chasing after the untrustworthy. It's time to take charge and show Crystal the exit sign.

The Triumph of Enforcement

Through these uproarious tales, the true power of enforcement shines bright. The once-enabling landlord has transformed into an enforcer of rules, and the results are nothing short of comedic gold. As I bid farewell to the late rent sagas, I revel in the newfound freedom from headaches and the delightful vacancy-filling dance ahead.

This chapter has regaled us with the sidesplitting chronicles of enabling tenants and the triumphant transformation into an enforcer of rules. With laughter as our guide, we navigate the unpredictable world of landlordship, armed with the knowledge that enforcement and comedy go hand in hand.

Chapter 26:
The Hilarious Dance of
Tenant Friendships

"I thought you are my friend, Mr. Landlord!"

Get ready for a laughter-filled ride as we explore the comedic side of tenant-landlord relationships. In this chapter, we'll discover why it's crucial to maintain professional boundaries and keep personal lives separate from the business of running properties. Brace yourselves for amusing tales of tenants attempting to befriend their landlord for special treatment, only to be met with a firm and humorous reality check.

Ah, the delicate balance between personal connections and professional boundaries. As a landlord, it's essential to remember that renting out properties is a business endeavor, not a quest for lifelong friendships. Cue the laughter, my friends, as we embark on a journey filled with tenants' attempts to forge special bonds and the landlord's clever navigation through the minefield of misplaced expectations.

Enter our main character, the charming tenant who believed friendship could be a shortcut to special privileges. Ignoring the clear boundaries, he failed to pay his rent online, triggering our protagonist's swift and humorous response. In a desperate plea, he approached me with the infamous line, "I thought you are my friend! How could you do this to me?" Oh, the hilarity that ensued!

In the face of this emotional plea, our unyielding landlord responded with calm wit and unshakeable resolve. "No sir," I retorted, a twinkle of amusement in my eyes, "You did this to yourself. If you had simply paid your rent on time, as you agreed to, none of this would have happened." The punchline? "I am not your friend; I am your landlord." The courtroom showdown was imminent, but our determined tenant, realizing the futility of his plea, decided to move out voluntarily the very next day. Victory through comedy!

Through this hilarious encounter, we witness the power of maintaining professional boundaries. Laughter echoes through the corridors of landlordship as we learn that personal connections should not influence the business decisions that must be made. The lesson here? Friendships are treasured in the appropriate setting, but professionalism prevails when it comes to renting properties.

This chapter has regaled us with the comedic escapades of tenants attempting to blur the lines between friendship and business. We've witnessed the triumph of professionalism and the laughter accompanying a well-delivered reality check. Always remember the fine art of balancing personal connections and the world of rental properties.

Chapter 27:
Lost in Translation - The Hilarious World of Texting Tenants

"What? You don't know how to text?"

Here, we delve into the humorous world of texting tenants and the laughter that ensues when communication becomes a comedy of errors. Join us as we explore the challenges landlords face when dealing with applicants unfamiliar or unwilling to embrace the art of texting.

As a savvy landlord, I understand the power and efficiency of communicating with tenants via text. But alas, not all applicants share the same level of enthusiasm or technical prowess regarding this modern form of communication. Get ready for hilarity as we encounter applicants who are lost in the world of texting or stubbornly resistant to the text-based revolution.

Picture this: a prospective tenant arrives with hope and dreams of finding a new home. But when asked to communicate through text, their confusion becomes palpable. "What? You don't know how to text on your phone?" I, caught in the midst of this communication conundrum, must make a difficult decision. Despite the potential loss of income, I opt not to accept tenants who are unable or unwilling to embrace the simplicity of texting. While some may see missed opportunities, I find solace in knowing that the ease and efficiency of texting outweigh any monetary gain lost. After all, a peaceful vacation thousands of miles away is far more enticing than deciphering archaic communication methods.

This chapter teaches us the importance of embracing modern communication methods. The laughs are aplenty as we witness the comedic struggles of tenants attempting to navigate the world of texting. From the lost-in-translation applicants to the stubbornly resistant, the message is clear: efficiency and ease are paramount in the landlord's world. Now, we bid farewell to the amusing tales of texting mishaps and miscommunications. In this age of technology, embracing efficient communication methods can lead to smoother interactions and even more enjoyable vacations.

Chapter 28:
"What? He's already late on rent? But he just moved in!"

A new tenant steps into our cherished rental property, full of hope and promise. Yet, before we can even catch our breath, trouble comes knocking. To our astonishment, this freshly arrived tenant fails to uphold their end of the bargain and falls behind on their rent. We're left scratching our heads and exclaiming, "But he just moved in!"

Here, we explore the landlord's conundrum when confronted with an early bird troublemaker. Do we dismiss their late payment as a minor blip or take immediate action to address the issue? As fellow landlords, we understand the significance of swift intervention. Recognizing the potential for further complications or damage, we tackle trouble head-on.

Now we just need to take charge and set the tone. So comes the undeniable power of proactive measures in preserving order and safeguarding our property. Rather than allowing the situation to fester, we opt to confront the issue directly, ensuring the tenant comprehends the importance of timely rent payment and adherence to the rules.

This chapter imparts valuable lessons as we navigate the early stages of a tenancy. Troublesome tenants often reveal their true colors from the start, and by taking immediate action, we can mitigate future challenges. Let this chapter be a reminder that being proactive, even if it means making tough decisions early on, is vital for maintaining a harmonious landlord-tenant relationship.

As we conclude this chapter, we bid farewell to the early bird troublemaker and reflect upon the invaluable lessons acquired. Let us embrace the power of swift action, knowing it paves the way for peace and prosperity within our rental properties.

Chapter 29:
The Google Review Threat

"You better return my deposit, or I'll write you a bad review on Google."

Once upon a time, in the exciting realm of landlordship, I was caught in a whirlwind of tenant troubles. Just when I thought I had seen it all, a tenant, let's call her Trouble-Maker Tina, pulled a stunt that left me rolling my eyes and shaking my head in disbelief.

You see, Trouble-Maker Tina decided to leave without a single word of notice, disregarding our sacred lease agreement. As a responsible landlord, I naturally held on to her security deposit, which was rightfully ours. Little did I know I was about to embark on a wild ride of threats and online review warfare.

One fateful day, my phone rang, and on the other end of the line was Trouble-Maker Tina herself. With a venomous tone, she unleashed her ultimatum, "You better give me my deposit, or I'll make sure the world knows how terrible you are through a scathing review on Google!"

Now, my fellow landlords, let me tell you—I am not one to back down from a challenge. With a mischievous grin, I responded, "Oh, my dear Trouble-Maker Tina, you're more than welcome to write whatever your heart desires. But rest assured, that deposit is staying right where it belongs!"

As I've learned throughout my adventures in the landlord realm, online reviews can be a double-edged sword. They have the power to make or break our reputations, but I refuse to let them dictate my worth as a landlord. Instead, I focus on providing top-notch service, maintaining open lines of communication, and ensuring my properties are in tip-top shape.

In this wacky world of online reviews, I've come to realize that disgruntled tenants are often the ones who shout the loudest. They take to the virtual stage to air their grievances while the satisfied ones quietly enjoy their comfortable dwellings. It's a circus of opinions out there, my friends, and I'm just a humble ringmaster juggling tenant concerns with a dash of landlord charm.

Now, I won't deny that negative reviews can sting a little. But as I ride this wild rollercoaster of landlordship, I've learned to find the humor in it all. Behind every angry rant lies an opportunity to showcase my professionalism and dedication in the face of adversity.

So, Trouble-Maker Tina, with all due respect, write your review if it brings you solace. But remember, my dear tenant, that your actions spoke louder than any online rant ever could. While you threatened to tarnish my name, I stood firm, knowing that I had upheld our agreement and acted within my rights as a landlord.

Ultimately, Trouble-Maker Tina may have moved on to another dwelling, but I remained steadfast. I took solace in knowing I had stood my ground, refusing to be swayed by empty threats. For, my fellow landlords, it is not the reviews that define us, but rather the character we display in the face of adversity.

Chapter 30:
The Unexpected Encounter

"Do you know who you are messing with?"

Ah, the life of a landlord—a never-ending journey filled with surprises and unexpected encounters. Allow me to regale you with a tale from my early days as a novice landlord when I had an encounter that left me both astonished and grateful for my quick thinking.

It was a dark and stormy night—well, maybe not stormy, but definitely past the acceptable hours for a rowdy party. A phone call shattered the tranquility as I sat in my cozy office, sipping my evening tea. It was a tenant lamenting about their neighbor's raucous gathering and blasting music well into the night. As a fresh-faced landlord eager to resolve issues promptly, I made a fateful decision—I would personally visit the noisy neighbor and request a reduction in volume.

Now, my dear readers, let me pause the tale momentarily and admit my naivety. Little did I know that this seemingly simple encounter would be anything but ordinary. Armed with determination and a polite smile, I made my way to the troublesome tenant's door, brimming with the confidence of a fledgling landlord.

As I knocked on the door, I braced myself for a potentially tense conversation. To my surprise, the door swung open, revealing a sight that could only be described as a scene from a circus. The tiny one-bedroom apartment, no more than 800 square feet, was bursting at the seams with at least 30 people—a lively gathering that seemed to defy the laws of spatial limitations.

The air was thick with the unmistakable scent of marijuana, and a hint of alcohol wafted from the tenant's breath. Undeterred by the overwhelming atmosphere, I mustered my best authoritative voice and kindly asked the tenant to lower the music due to the late hour.

To my astonishment, the tenant responded with a menacing sneer and said, "Don't tell me what to do. Do you know who you are messing with?" In a chilling display, he opened his jacket to reveal a gun strapped to his side—a sight that sent shivers down my spine.

Dear readers, I must confess that I momentarily lost my cool. But in that critical moment, I summoned my wits and recognized the importance of my safety above all else. Without speaking, I turned on my heels and swiftly retreated from the perilous encounter.

As I safely distanced myself from the tenant's abode, I felt relief wash over me. It was abundantly clear that I needed to take swift action to protect myself and my other tenants from such an unpredictable and potentially dangerous individual.

With a steely resolve, I immediately drafted a 30-day notice for the troublesome tenant to vacate the premises. The following day, I hand-delivered the notice, ensuring that my intentions were unmistakable—that the path ahead for this tenant no longer intersected with my humble abode.

And so, dear readers, the tale of the unexpected encounter reached its conclusion. It is a powerful reminder that landlords navigate a world filled with diverse characters and unforeseen challenges. While we must address issues and foster a harmonious living environment, we must always prioritize our safety and well-being.

As I continue to tread the path of landlordship, this encounter serves as a valuable lesson—a reminder that resilience, quick thinking, and a dash of caution are the keys to maintaining a thriving rental community. So, my fellow landlords, let us proceed with vigilance, ensuring the safety and tranquility of our domains while preserving our peace of mind.

Chapter 31:
The Case of the Secretive Canine

"What dog? I don't have a dog."

In the intricate web of landlordship, we often encounter tenants who push the boundaries, hoping to bend the rules to their advantage. One such situation arose when a tenant attempted to sneak a furry friend into my pet-free property—a tale that left me perplexed and determined to uphold the sanctity of my lease agreements.

It all began innocently enough. The tenant had signed the lease agreement, fully aware of the strict pet policy. However, as time passed, whispers circulated among fellow tenants—a rumor of a clandestine canine within my property's walls. As a vigilant landlord, I swiftly investigated to uncover the truth.

One fateful afternoon, I spotted the tenant strolling through the complex with a small, four-legged companion by his side—an undeniable confirmation of the rumors that had reached my ears. Summoning all my courage, I approached the tenant, ready to address the violation head-on.

With an air of feigned innocence, I confronted him, pointing out the obvious presence of a dog in his unit. His response? A brazen denial, as if attempting to gaslight me into questioning my own eyes and senses. "What dog? I don't have a dog," he exclaimed, his voice dripping with faux confusion. My patience worn thin; I saw through his ruse and realized that swift action was necessary to maintain the integrity of my property.

Determined to uphold the rules I had set forth, I decided that this tenant could no longer reside within the confines of my rental domain. However, I also recognized the challenges of pursuing legal action to prove the violation in court. Gathering evidence required invasive surveillance and the uncertainty of an outcome that could easily be disputed.

In a stroke of strategic thinking, I opted for a different approach. Instead of engaging in a protracted battle, I chose not to renew the tenant's lease, giving him a 30-day notice to seek alternative accommodations. By taking this course of action, I could swiftly remove the tenant without the need for irrefutable evidence of the dog's presence.

But the lessons learned from this incident extended far beyond the resolution itself. It served as a stark reminder that maintaining the respect and authority of a landlord is paramount to maintaining order within a rental community. The eyes of the other tenants were upon me, eagerly observing my response to the violation. If I exhibited weakness or falter in my resolve, the consequences could be dire—an unraveling of the delicate fabric that holds a complex together.

In the intricate dance of landlord-tenant relationships, it is imperative to take swift and decisive action when faced with rule violations. By doing so, we not only protect the integrity of our property but also send a clear message to other tenants that the rules are not negotiable.

So, my fellow landlords, let us stand firm in the face of such challenges. Uphold the principles laid out in our lease agreements, and remember that by taking the necessary steps to address violations promptly, we maintain harmony and order within our rental communities.

As we continue our journey through the labyrinthine world of landlordship, may this tale serve as a reminder that strength, determination, and adherence to our principles are the keys to navigating the unpredictable terrain of tenant interactions.

Chapter 32:
Ensuring Legal Safety with Ambiguity

"Why are you kicking me out?"

In the intricate realm of landlordship, some moments call for swift and decisive action, leaving tenants perplexed and seeking answers as to why they are being unceremoniously handed their notice to vacate. During these encounters, the delicate dance between landlord and tenant reaches a critical juncture that requires careful navigation to protect one's interests while maintaining a veil of enigmatic authority.

Picture this scene: A tenant, faced with the unsettling news of impending departure, musters the courage to approach me, their perplexed expression demanding an explanation. "Why are you kicking me out?" they inquire, their voice tinged with confusion and frustration. "What did I do wrong?"

In this delicate moment, my response remains steadfast, delivered with detached finality. "Well, you are on a month-to-month lease, and the owners have decided not to renew your lease," I calmly explain, carefully choosing my words. "As for the reasons behind their decision, we prefer not to divulge those specifics. Good luck to you in finding alternative accommodations."

This exchange may appear cold and aloof to an outsider, lacking in the compassion one might expect. However, as seasoned landlords, we understand the calculated reasoning behind such an approach. While the tenant yearns for answers, we are not obligated to provide them with ammunition that could be used against us in a court of law.

A wise landlord understands the potential legal implications of divulging specific reasons for eviction. With the advent of audio recorders tucked away in pockets and purses, we must exercise caution in our responses, ensuring we do not inadvertently provide grounds for legal action. Each word we utter carries the weight of potential consequence, a potential trap waiting to be sprung.

In this intricate dance of landlord-tenant relationships, the power of silence cannot be overstated. We maintain a guarded demeanor, shielding ourselves from the prying ears and recording devices that may seek to exploit our words. By offering minimal information, we protect our interests and maintain a shield of legal prudence.

Tenants may be bewildered by our refusal to disclose the exact reasons for their eviction. They may feel slighted, searching for answers that remain frustratingly out of reach. Yet, in our silence lies the power to protect ourselves from potential legal entanglements and ensure our actions are rooted in legal and contractual obligations.

As we traverse the intricate landscape of landlordship, let us remember the delicate balance we must strike. While compassion and understanding have their place, protecting our rights and the integrity of our position cannot be compromised. By embracing the art of discretion, we navigate the complexities of tenant interactions with poise and wisdom.

Chapter 33:
Smile! The Camera's Watchful Eye

Within property management, one encounters a diverse array of tenants, each with unique quirks and idiosyncrasies. Occasionally, we stumble upon a tenant whose behavior veers into the realm of the peculiar, leaving us questioning their motives and mental state. Such was the case with a tenant who, unbeknownst to me then, developed an uncanny obsession with recording the repair process within her apartment.

Let me set the stage for you: A tenant notorious for submitting work orders at an astonishing frequency would eagerly welcome the repairman into her abode. However, instead of providing the customary assistance or guidance, she would trail the repairman's every move, clutching her smartphone like a lifeline. A constant video recording ensued, capturing every twist of the wrench and every turn of the screw.

Naturally, my curiosity was piqued, and I felt compelled to address this peculiar behavior. I approached her, questioning the purpose behind her meticulous documentation. With a hint of unease, she explained that it was for her own protection. Bewilderment washed over me as I struggled to comprehend the reasoning behind such extreme caution.

It became evident that this tenant's peculiar conduct stemmed from deeper issues. Her erratic behavior and her nomadic history of apartment hopping hinted at a mental instability that had gone unnoticed. It was a realization that brought forth a new understanding—an understanding that dealing with individuals who are mentally disabled requires a nuanced approach.

In navigating the complexities of mental disabilities, my subsequent encounters with mentally disabled tenants taught me a valuable lesson: sometimes, avoidance is the best course of action. Rather than engaging in prolonged communication or attempting to address their unique needs, it is often wiser to maintain a respectful distance. Doing so minimizes the risk of exacerbating their condition or inadvertently causing distress.

It is essential to remember that the responsibility for providing adequate care and support to mentally disabled individuals lies outside the realm of our expertise as landlords. Our role is to provide safe and habitable living conditions, but navigating their mental health intricacies is beyond our purview.

So, when faced with mentally disabled tenants, it is best to adopt a hands-off approach. This does not mean we should neglect our responsibilities or deny them the assistance they may require, but rather, we should exercise caution and seek guidance from appropriate professionals who possess the knowledge and expertise to provide the care these individuals deserve.

In the case of our tenant, I accepted that her compulsion to record every repair visit was not a reflection of personal animosity or ill intentions. It was merely a manifestation of her unique struggles. By acknowledging her mental condition and respecting her boundaries, I maintained professionalism and ensured that her needs were met without inadvertently causing harm. So, my fellow landlords, let us approach the enigmatic world of mental disabilities with compassion and understanding. Let us recognize the limits of our role and seek the guidance of professionals who can provide the necessary support. By embracing a hands-off approach and treating each tenant with respect, we can navigate these delicate situations with empathy, ensuring a harmonious and inclusive environment for all.

Chapter 34:
Change Begins with Action

In the vast tapestry of tenants that grace our rental properties, we encounter a wide spectrum of behaviors, ranging from model citizens to those who seem destined to test the limits of our patience. It is a reality of this business that some individuals, particularly new tenants, may arrive with a set of issues that can escalate over time. As landlords, it is our duty to address these concerns head-on and effect change before the situation worsens.

One common issue that arises is damage to the property. Whether it's a broken window or a gaping hole in the wall, it is crucial to address these damages swiftly and ensure tenants take responsibility for their actions. Waiting until they move out, hoping that they will rectify the damages, is a recipe for disappointment and an unnecessary financial burden. It is far better to take proactive steps and compel tenants to pay for damages immediately, preventing further deterioration of the property and minimizing future expenses.

Furthermore, when a tenant or their children begin to exhibit troublesome behavior, it is imperative to act decisively. No warning should be necessary. By swiftly issuing a 30-day non-renewal notice, we clearly communicate that their actions will not be tolerated within our community. This may seem harsh, particularly when considering the circumstances of a long-time tenant whose child has fallen into delinquency. However, it is essential to remember that empathy for bad behavior only reinforces it and ultimately harms us.

I recall an instance involving a single mother who had been a tenant for many years. When she initially moved in, her child was well-behaved and showed promise. However, as he reached the age of eleven, he became entangled in the influence of local gangs, transforming into a troublesome presence within the community. Graffiti adorned the walls, and common areas fell victim to his destructive whims. Despite repeated warnings to the mother, her pleas for leniency, and my desire to see the good in her, I ultimately had to face the harsh reality.

The damage's true extent became painfully apparent the day they vacated the premises. The apartment bore the scars of their reckless existence, and rehabilitation costs soared to two months' worth of time and over $3000 in expenses. It was a sobering lesson that reminded me of the importance of maintaining a firm stance when confronted with problematic tenants. Empathy, when misplaced and misdirected, becomes an instrument of self-inflicted cruelty.

Let us not be perpetual suckers, swayed by sob stories and empty promises. While we may sympathize with the struggles faced by tenants living on minimum wage, it is essential to recognize when we are being taken advantage of. Laughing behind our backs, they revel in our perceived gullibility, joking about our naivety. It is our duty to break free from this cycle of exploitation, refusing to allow ourselves to be the punchline of their deceptions.

Instead, let us embrace a mindset of self-preservation, guided by a keen awareness of the realities of our profession. We must be unyielding in holding tenants accountable for their actions, promptly addressing damages, and taking decisive action when faced with disruptive behavior. By doing so, we create an environment that fosters respect, responsibility, and mutual trust—a community where most tenants thrive, while those who seek to undermine it find themselves without a place to call home.

Remember, change begins with action. Through our unwavering commitment to maintaining the integrity of our properties and protecting our own interests, we shape the future of our rental business. So, my fellow landlords, let us shed the shackles of misplaced empathy and embrace a stance of firm resolve. Only then can we ensure the prosperity of our investments and preserve the sanctity

Chapter 35:
Prioritizing Peace of Mind

Ah, the familiar plea of a tenant seeking redemption. "Please give me another chance," they implore, promising to pay their rent on time. It is a scene that has played out countless times in the realm of landlordship. But let us not be swayed by empty promises or the allure of potential change. The truth is troublemakers and chronic late-payers are not worth sacrificing our precious time and well-being.

We must recognize that our time and health are invaluable commodities. Losing sleep over a problematic tenant is a sure sign that action must be taken. Why endure restless nights and unnecessary stress when the solution is within our grasp? By immediately giving notice to troublesome tenants, we liberate ourselves from the burden they impose upon us. There is no need to wait until they pay their rent; their departure is the ultimate goal. Grant them notice today and watch as the weight on our shoulders begins to lift.

People, dear landlords, rarely change their ways. We cannot hold onto false hope, believing that a simple promise will suddenly transform a chronic late-payer into a model tenant. The reality is that if we choose to keep such individuals within our midst, we will only find ourselves dwelling upon the issue for months or even years. Is a meager sum of money worth sacrificing our peace of mind, sleep, and health? I think not.

Let us remember that our well-being should always take precedence. It is not selfishness but rather self-preservation. Our mental and physical health are priceless commodities that cannot be quantified in monetary terms. So, when faced with the choice between losing sleep and our own peace of mind, the answer becomes clear. The bad seed must be uprooted promptly, allowing us to reclaim our tranquility and regain our zest for life.

We must never underestimate the toll that troublesome tenants can take on our well-being. The constant worry, the sleepless nights, the nagging sense of unease all add up, eroding our happiness and fulfillment. Is this truly the life we envisioned for ourselves as landlords? The answer is a resounding no.

Therefore, let us not hesitate to prioritize our own peace of mind. Let us release ourselves from the clutches of troublesome tenants and embrace the freedom of a clean slate. In doing so, we create space for new, responsible individuals who will honor their commitments and treat our properties respectfully. It is a win-win scenario—an opportunity for us to regain control of our lives and ensure the harmony of our rental ventures.

Remember, dear landlords, you hold the power to shape your destiny. It is within your hands to create an environment that nurtures your well-being and allows your investments to flourish. Do not be swayed by empty promises or the notion that people can change overnight. Trust your instincts, prioritize your peace of mind, and watch your rental business thrive under your wise guidance.

Let us embark on this journey with a renewed focus on our happiness and contentment. May the days of sleepless nights and tenant-induced stress become a distant memory, replaced by a sense of tranquility and fulfillment. The path to success as landlords lies not in sacrificing our well-being but in safeguarding it with unwavering determination.

Chapter 36:
The Art of Silence

Ah, the familiar sound of excuses, spinning tales of lost phones and unforeseen circumstances. As landlords, we have become masters at deciphering the truth hidden beneath layers of deceit. When tenants fail to pay their rent on time and conveniently avoid our calls and messages, it is crucial to see through their charades. Behind their silence lies a purposeful intention—either they lack the funds, or they seek greener pastures elsewhere, leaving us, the unsuspecting landlords, in the lurch.

But fear not, dear landlords, for we hold the power to navigate these treacherous waters with finesse. Reading between the lines becomes our superpower, allowing us to avoid becoming hapless victims of their elaborate ruses. No longer shall we succumb to their endless excuses, nor waste precious time awaiting their call or response. Instead, we shall take charge and protect our interests.

The path to dealing with such tenants lies in the art of effective communication. A simple text message shall serve as the catalyst, notifying the tenant that eviction proceedings will commence on a specific date should their silence persist. By setting this ultimatum, we free ourselves from the futile pursuit of an unlikely response. A swift call back will ensue if the tenant desires to remain in our property. However, if their intentions lie elsewhere, the sound of their silence shall echo until the fateful day of the eviction hearing.

As landlords, we must embrace a steadfast mentality that recognizes our role is not that of a debt collector. It is not our duty to chase after delinquent tenants, desperately seeking restitution for our lost revenue. Instead, we understand that the one who speaks the least often emerges victorious. Silence becomes our weapon of choice, leaving the burden of communication on their shoulders.

Take, for instance, the tale of Arely, a tenant who danced around her responsibilities. Countless messages were left unanswered in the hopes of a resolution. Yet, on the third day of the month, after three days of fruitless attempts, a simple text message was sent—a subtle reminder that eviction loomed unless the full amount and accompanying fees were paid within two days. And what happened next? Ah, the sweet sound of her immediate reply, riddled with excuses and pleas for leniency. But did we, as wise landlords, engage in a lengthy back-and-forth? No, we chose the power of silence, ignoring her words and watching as the full sum magically appeared the very next day.

In our dealings with tenants, we must discern when to speak and when to hold our tongues. We, the landlords, possess the ultimate leverage, for it is said that he who holds the gold makes the rules. Thus, we confidently wield this power, understanding that our silence can be more potent than any carefully crafted response.

We need not waste our breath or precious time chasing after tenants who play games with our livelihoods. Instead, we employ the strength of our position to set boundaries and demand accountability. By recognizing our power, we navigate the intricate dance of landlordship with grace and authority.

So, let us don our mantle of silence, speaking only when necessary and allowing our actions to speak louder than words. Tales of lost phones or feeble excuses shall not sway us. Our path is clear—to protect our interests and assert our authority as landlords. And in doing so, we shall rise above the noise, securing our rightful place as masters of our rental realms.

Chapter 37:
The Art of Selective
Communication

Ah, the ever-ringing phone, that relentless beast demanding our attention day and night. But fear not, my fellow landlords, for I have discovered the secret to maintaining our sanity and preserving our precious time. It lies in selective communication—a dance between text messages, strategic responses, and the witty wisdom of knowing when to pick up the phone.

Now, let's get to the heart of the matter, shall we? As landlords, we all know only two reasons warrant our attention: rent payment issues and the eternal quest for repairs. Everything else? Let's just say it often falls into the realm of pure nonsense. I mean, seriously, do they really expect us to drop everything and rush to change a lightbulb? Can't they just use a chair or ask their super strong, lightbulb-changing neighbor, Hercules? Ah, the audacity!

But here's the genius part: when tenants decide to unleash their requests and queries via text message, we gain the upper hand. We become the masters of our own communication destiny. We can carefully choose which messages to respond to, like a curator selecting the finest art for an exhibition, and which ones to simply let fade into the abyss of digital oblivion. Let me tell you, dear landlords, approximately 80% of the time, it's all just an elaborate performance of verbal acrobatics, a circus act of pointless banter.

And when we do respond, we must do so with flair, brevity, and a dash of wit. Our texts become our weapons of linguistic delight, designed to inform and entertain. By keeping our replies short and to the point, we convey our efficiency and give tenants a subtle reminder that we are not there to engage in lengthy debates about the existence of unicorns or the mysteries of quantum physics. Nope, we're here to get things done, my friends!

Now, let's talk about timing. Oh, the sweet art of delay! Weave a magical web of expectation and urgency by establishing a rule that we only respond to texts twice a day—at the glorious hours of 10 a.m. and 4 p.m.. Tenants soon learn that we are not at their beck and call, readily available to solve their every trivial issue. No, no, no! We are the enigmatic landlords, the masters of our schedule, the elusive beings they can't quite pin down. By delaying our responses, we create a sense of wonder and intrigue. They begin to wonder, "Will I receive a response today? Or will my inquiry be lost in the vast expanse of cyberspace?"

Ah, and let us not forget the wonders of human laziness. People have an uncanny ability to find solutions when left to their own devices. It's as if a hidden wellspring of resourcefulness awakens within them. When they can't find us to voice their concerns, they embark on the grand adventure of solving problems themselves. Suddenly, they discover the hidden talents of lightbulb replacement, plumbing wizardry, and even the mystical art of hanging curtains. Who knew they had it in them? And all it took was a slight delay in our text responses to unlock their inner superheroes.

So, dear landlords, let us revel in the joy of selective communication. Let us dance to the rhythm of text messages, responding with wit and brevity, all while maintaining the illusion of being elusive beings who control time itself. Embrace the power of delayed responses and witness the magic of tenants finding their own solutions. We shall navigate the communication realm with grace, humor, and the satisfaction of knowing that we have preserved our time and sanity in the process.

Remember, my fellow landlords, the path to efficient communication lies in mastering the art of selection. Rent payment issues and necessary repairs take center stage while nonsense becomes a mere sideshow. So pick up that phone, read that text, and unleash your inner landlord wizardry. Your tenants may not know it, but they're about to witness the most entertaining, efficient, and slightly enigmatic communication they've ever experienced. Cheers to reclaiming our time and having a few laughs along the way!

Chapter 38:
Holy Grail of Month-to-Month Lease

As a landlord, I've had my fair share of experiences when it comes to lease agreements. Let me regale you with a tale that will make you question the traditional wisdom of signing a minimum one-year lease and have you laughing at the absurdity of it all.

Picture this: I had a tenant who seemed like the perfect match on paper. They passed all the background checks, their references were stellar, and their credit score could make any landlord's heart skip a beat. Naturally, I thought signing them up for a one-year lease would guarantee me a peaceful and trouble-free rental period. Oh, how wrong I was!

Soon after this model tenant moved in, I discovered they had an uncanny ability to transform into a nocturnal DJ. Yes, you heard that right. At the stroke of midnight, they would unleash a symphony of thumping beats, blaring music, and the occasional ear-piercing rendition of karaoke. My neighbors, who were initially friendly and understanding, quickly turned into a disgruntled mob armed with pitchforks and torches.

Now, you may wonder, "Can't you just take this tenant to court for violating the lease agreement?" Well, my friend, that's where things get interesting. As I sought legal advice from numerous eviction experts, I discovered that proving noise violations in court can be as challenging as nailing jelly to a tree. The judges seemed to have a knack for requiring video evidence of the disturbances and the occasional witness testimony. It felt like I was starring in my own absurd reality TV show, trying to capture the elusive DJ tenant in action.

The odds of winning such cases were as uncertain as a coin toss. I could have an extensive list of violations, but I found myself stuck between a rock and a hard place without solid evidence. The frustration was real, my friend.

However, as fate would have it, a wise attorney specializing in tenant management bestowed upon me the secret of lease agreements: the holy grail of month-to-month leases. With a gleam in their eye, they explained that my life would have been much simpler if I had signed a month-to-month lease with this particular tenant.

With a month-to-month lease, all it takes is a 30-day non-renewal notice. There is no need for court hearings or hair-pulling moments trying to gather evidence. It's as easy as telling the troublesome tenant, "Adieu, farewell, and please turn the volume down on your way out." A swift eviction without the legal circus.

Now, I know what you might be thinking. "But won't signing a one-year lease at least ensure that tenants stay put for a minimum of twelve months, thus reducing the vacancy rate?" Ah, my friend, that assumption couldn't be further from the truth. In this modern age, tenants possess an uncanny ability to vanish into thin air, leaving landlords scratching their heads in disbelief.

They don't care about breaking leases or leaving their deposit behind. It's as if a new trend has emerged where tenants see breaking leases as a mere inconvenience, akin to changing their socks or getting a new haircut. Sadly, it's bizarre, but it has become the norm in the rental world. So, let's cast aside the myth of the one-year lease and embrace the simplicity and flexibility of month-to-month agreements.

In conclusion, my fellow landlords, learn from my misadventures and consider the month-to-month lease as your new best friend. It offers the freedom to bid farewell to troublesome tenants without the headache of court battles, and it adapts to the whimsical nature of today's tenants. Embrace the change, break free from the shackles of tradition, and forge a path towards stress-free landlordship. Laughter is the best remedy; sometimes, the most absurd tales hold valuable lessons. Cheers to the wonders of month-to-month leases!

Chapter 39:
Dating in the Workplace

"Would you like to go out sometime?"

Ah, the perils of navigating the treacherous waters of mixing business and pleasure! As a seasoned landlord, I hold steadfast to my mantra: "Never eat when you eat!" In other words, keep business separate from personal affairs or risk facing a recipe for disaster. Let me regale you with a tale that perfectly exemplifies this principle.

Picture this: I had a tenant named Christy, a vibrant woman in her mid-thirties who happened to be a single mom with a remarkable talent for attracting colorful stories. She had four children, each a gift from a different father, making her life a mosaic of unexpected twists and turns. One fine day, my phone buzzed with an urgent text from Christy, insisting I call her back immediately. Ah, the allure of an emergency!

But being the wise and experienced landlord I am, I didn't fall into the trap of responding hastily. No, no, my friends! I let a full day pass, savoring the anticipation, knowing that emergencies seldom live up to their melodramatic hype. And indeed, as I picked up the phone the next day, I braced myself for an exaggerated tale that would rival even the most gripping telenovela plot.

As our conversation unfolded, I couldn't help but sense a shift in the atmosphere. Christy's inquiries about my well-being seemed oddly personal. Before I could even process what was happening, she casually suggested grabbing a cup of coffee together. Oh, the audacity! Clearly, this conversation had veered into dangerous territory, where business and personal interests collided like clumsy bumper cars at a fair.

Now, you might think any ordinary person would be over the moon at the prospect of dating a beautiful woman like Christy. But not I, my friend! I possess an unwavering commitment to professionalism and a knack for seeing the potential chaos beneath the surface. Venturing into personal relationships with tenants is like opening Pandora's box—a surefire recipe for sleepless nights and endless complications.

So, with the grace and charm of a seasoned landlord, I politely declined her invitation, thanking her for her interest but emphasizing the importance of maintaining clear boundaries. A momentary pause hung in the air before we bid each other adieu, and I couldn't help but pat myself on the back for my unwavering resolve. But before ending the call, my landlord instincts kicked in, and I couldn't resist slipping in a gentle reminder about the upcoming rent payment. After all, it's essential to keep the gears of business turning smoothly, even in the face of romantic entanglements.

In the end, my commitment to keeping business and pleasure separate protects the integrity of my landlord kingdom and ensures that I maintain a professional and amicable relationship with my tenants. So, let's raise a figurative cup of coffee (without any romantic undertones, of course) to the art of self-discipline and the comedic escapades that can arise when business and personal matters collide. Cheers!

Chapter 40:
Doing Favors for Tenants

"Can you do me a favor?"

Ah, the dreaded words that can send shivers down a landlord's spine. "Can you do me a favor?" It's a phrase that taught me the importance of sticking to my instincts and never bending over backward for anyone. In the realm of landlording, it's crucial to maintain a straightforward and uncomplicated tenant-landlord relationship. No favors, no exceptions.

Let me regale you with the tale of Mary, one of my tenants who recently welcomed a new addition to her family. Picture this: Mary, a single mom with a brood of four kids from three different dads, comes to me with a request. Her current one-bedroom unit is bursting at the seams, and she desperately needs more space. She pleads with me, "Please, Mr. Landlord, can you find it in your heart to let me move into a larger two-bedroom unit?"

Now, you might be thinking, "Why not give the poor woman a break? She's dealing with enough chaos as it is!" Well, my dear reader, let me take you on a journey into the intricacies of landlording.

My policy regarding tenant requests for transfers is crystal clear: I either reject the request outright or, if I do grant it, I impose a hefty cleaning fee. Moving an existing tenant from one unit to another is like navigating a treacherous minefield. It's not as simple as packing up a few boxes and hauling them across the hallway. Oh no, it's far more complicated than that.

When a tenant transfers units, I have to ensure that the new unit is cleaned and prepared for their arrival. This means investing thousands of dollars to spruce it up, making it a delightful and pristine living space. But wait, there's more! I also have to deal with the aftermath of the tenant vacating their previous unit. Trust me, it's not a pretty sight. There's cleaning, repairs, and the occasional bizarre discovery (I'll spare you the gory details).

So, armed with these insights, I had to make a decision regarding Mary's plea for a larger unit. Now, being a landlord who's been around the block a few times (figuratively, of course), I should have stuck to my guns and said, "Sorry, Mary, but the answer is no." But alas, there was a tiny voice in my head saying, "Maybe this time will be different. Perhaps Mary will be a grateful and responsible tenant who will keep her unit in tip-top shape."

Oh, how foolish I was! In a moment of uncharacteristic weakness, I decided to grant Mary's request without imposing my usual $500 cleaning fee. Yes, I tossed my rules out the window like a landlord playing landlord-themed basketball. Little did I know that this small act of kindness would set off a chain reaction of chaos and absurdity.

In no time, Mary settled into her new two-bedroom abode, seemingly content with her upgraded living space. But then, as if to test my patience and sanity, she threw a curveball at me—a curveball in the form of a furry, four-legged companion. Yes, my friends, Mary adopted a dog even though she knows it's against the rules. So I guess she assumed one favor would lead to another. Well, she assumed inaccurately as I filed for eviction the same day!

Today, I pride myself on being a firm but fair landlord. Rules are rules, and they apply to everyone. So, I did what any responsible landlord would do—I initiated eviction proceedings whenever I see fit. No favors, No exceptions.

Chapter 41:
Tenant Expectations

"You're supposed to buy me a new refrigerator!"

Ah, the delightful encounter with an entitled tenant who believes the world revolves around their every whim. Allow me to regale you with the tale of one such tenant who demanded everything but the kitchen sink—although I'm sure she would have asked for that too if she thought she could get away with it.

You see, my policy as a landlord is simple: I don't provide refrigerators in my apartments. Instead, I kindly request that new tenants bring their own. Most people understand and have no issue with it. Many prefer to use their own trusted appliances. However, there are always exceptions to the rule, and that's where our entitled tenant enters the picture.

This particular tenant had been on a government housing program for a staggering 20 years. She claimed to have a disability that prevented her from working, yet whenever I saw her, she seemed to be as fit as a fiddle—lifting heavy groceries and tirelessly tending to her yard. But I digress.

Years of receiving free handouts had cultivated a sense of entitlement within her. She believed that the world owed her everything and that anyone in her vicinity was obligated to bend over backward to fulfill her demands. It wasn't a matter of asking for a favor; it was a matter of demanding what she believed was rightfully hers.

And so it began—the never-ending requests for new appliances or tile replacements every time I crossed paths with her. I could feel my patience wearing thin with each encounter. How had I fallen victim to this perpetual cycle of entitlement?

Enough was enough. I had reached my breaking point and knew it was time to put my foot down. Summoning all the courage within me, I decided to confront her head-on. I looked her square in the eye and uttered the words that would forever echo in the annals of landlord-tenant history: "Lady, you're asking for all these changes, so I assume you're not very happy here. And that's just not acceptable. We want to ensure that you and your family live in perpetual happiness. So why don't you start looking for another place to live? I would be more than happy to waive the notice requirement and expedite your departure."

Silence filled the air as my words hung heavily between us. She seemed taken aback, her entitled façade momentarily shattered. Perhaps she hadn't expected such a direct response. Or maybe, just maybe, my proclamation had struck a chord within her, reminding her that her demands were unreasonable and unjust.

From that day forward, she ceased her incessant bothering. The frequent requests for new appliances and tile replacements vanished into thin air. It was as if a weight had been lifted off my shoulders— a weight composed of entitlement and unrealistic expectations.

You see, my dear reader, sometimes the only way to deal with an entitled tenant is to stand your ground and remind them that their demands are not a requirement but a privilege. It's crucial to maintain the balance of power and not let yourself become a doormat for their unreasonable requests.

In the end, this encounter taught me a valuable lesson. It reinforced the importance of setting boundaries and asserting my authority as a landlord. It also reminded me that not everyone will appreciate the efforts we make or the accommodations we provide.

So, to all the landlords facing similar challenges, remember this: You have the power to say no and protect your sanity. Don't let entitlement seep into your domain. Stand tall, set your boundaries, and maintain the balance in the tenant-landlord dance. And may your encounters with entitled tenants become amusing anecdotes to share with fellow landlords over a glass of wine or a pint of laughter.

Chapter 42:
Never-Ending Excuses

"I Just Lost My Job, Can You Help Me?"

Ah, the timeless plea for assistance from a tenant in distress. It seems that life has thrown yet another curveball, and they're desperately seeking a lifeline to help them stay afloat. But as a seasoned landlord, I've learned that navigating these requests requires careful consideration and a keen eye for self-preservation.

Imagine this scenario: a tenant approaches me, a sense of desperation evident in their voice, and pleads, "I just lost my job. Can you help me apply for emergency assistance where a local agency would cover my upcoming rent, dude?" Their plea may tug at my heartstrings, but it's crucial to remember that my role as a landlord is to protect my interests and maintain a profitable business.

My experience has taught me never to sign my name on such paperwork. Let me tell you why. The government, bless its bureaucratic heart, operates on its own timetable. It could take a daunting 2 to 3 months for any rental assistance request to wade through the labyrinth of red tape and reach a resolution. But here's the kicker—the rent is due on the first of August, and it's the tenant's responsibility to pay on time.

If I were to put my signature on that rental assistance application, I would effectively surrender my rights as a landlord. I'd be at the agency's mercy, waiting for them to process the payment—likely no earlier than October or November. In the meantime, I've relinquished my right to evict the tenant, even if they fail to uphold their end of the bargain.

And let's not forget that there's always the possibility of the application being rejected. If that were to happen, I would find myself in a nightmarish predicament—losing out on 3 to 4 months' worth of rent money and being forced to shell out additional funds to evict said tenant. It's a lose-lose proposition, my friend, and one I'm not willing to entertain.

As much as I empathize with the struggles tenants face, I must prioritize my financial stability and risk mitigation. While I may genuinely want to assist this tenant, I refuse to do so at the expense of my own livelihood. It's simply too great a risk to expose myself to.

So, with a polite but firm "No, thanks," I decline their request. I encourage them to explore other avenues for assistance, such as seeking employment or reaching out to local organizations that specialize in providing support during tough times. It's not that I lack compassion, but rather, I recognize the importance of maintaining a business mindset and protecting my own interests.

In the intricate dance between compassion and self-preservation, finding the right balance is paramount. As landlords, we must weigh the potential risks and rewards, always considering the long-term implications of our decisions. And while it's never easy to say no, sometimes it's the wisest choice we can make.

So, my fellow landlords, stand strong in your resolve, knowing that your decisions are guided by sound judgment and the pursuit of a thriving rental business. May your encounters with tenants in need remind you of the delicate equilibrium we must maintain, and may you navigate these situations with tact and pragmatism.

Chapter 43:
Dealing with Insurance Companies

"Oh My God, the Recent Dust Storm!"

Dust storms. Those relentless forces of nature can wreak havoc on even the sturdiest of roofs. As a landlord with properties in an area prone to these dusty tempests, I've learned to take precautions and ensure that my insurance policy covers such incidents. And let me tell you, my friend, the dusty adventures I've had with insurance companies are nothing short of epic tales filled with humor, frustration, and valuable life lessons.

Picture this: It was the summer of multiple consecutive dust storms, hitting my area like a relentless barrage of sandpaper. It was as if Mother Nature had decided to throw a wild party, with dust swirling and billowing everywhere. I watched in awe as trees disappeared, houses became indistinguishable from the surrounding desert, and even the air seemed to have taken on a sandy tint. It was like living in a post-apocalyptic world but with a touch of comedic chaos.

Now, amidst this meteorological madness, one of my apartment unit roofs suffered damage. It was as if the dust demons had aimed specifically at my property, unleashing their full fury upon that poor roof. I stood there, hands on hips, surveying the damage with exasperation and admiration for nature's power.

Naturally, I had to file a claim with my insurance company. Armed with determination and skepticism, I picked up the phone and dialed their number. Little did I know that this simple act would kickstart a battle of wits and patience that would put the Trojan War to shame.

When I uttered, "I need to file a claim," an invisible line was drawn. It was as if a switch had been flipped, and suddenly, the insurance company morphed into a formidable adversary. Gone were the friendly customer service representatives who would cheerfully answer questions and process paperwork. In their place stood claims adjusters armed with skepticism, fine print, and an unwavering determination to pay as little as possible.

The first lesson I learned in this dust-covered odyssey was the importance of meticulous documentation. The insurance company's mantra seemed to be, "If it's not on paper, it didn't happen." Every conversation, every email, every detail had to be recorded. It was like playing a real-life game of Clue, except instead of solving a murder, I was trying to piece together a puzzle of dusty destruction.

As days turned into weeks, and my phone bills skyrocketed, I found myself diving headfirst into the world of insurance jargon. Deductibles, coverage limits, depreciation, and all those other fancy terms danced in front of my eyes like a demented circus. It was like learning a new language, except this language seemed to have been specifically designed to confuse and confound.

But amidst the frustration and confusion, moments of absurdity provided comic relief like the time I was put on hold for what felt like an eternity, only to be transferred to another department that promptly put me on hold again. It was a never-ending loop of elevator music and robotic voices assuring me that my call was important to them. By the time I finally spoke to a live person, I had started composing a symphony in my head using the tune of that godforsaken hold music.

And let's not forget the joy of dealing with claims adjusters who seemed to possess an uncanny ability to make even the most straightforward situation sound like an unsolvable riddle. Their responses were filled with vague statements, contradictory information, and an air of superiority that would make even the most seasoned detective scratch their head in bewilderment. I half-expected them to start quoting Sherlock Holmes or reciting riddles worthy of the Sphinx.

But amidst the bureaucratic labyrinth, I discovered an essential truth: the insurance company's job is to pay as little as possible, or better yet not pay at all. It's a harsh reality that can leave even the most patient and level-headed individuals feeling frustrated and defeated. Yet, armed with the knowledge that I wasn't alone in this battle, I persevered.

I reached out to fellow landlords, forming a support group of sorts. We swapped stories, shared tips, and even developed a secret handshake (okay, maybe not the last part, but you get the idea). It was a lifeline in the stormy sea of insurance claims, a reminder that we were all in this together, armed with nothing but our wits and a burning desire to protect our investments.

Amid this arduous journey, I discovered a powerful weapon that turned the tide in my favor: documentation. Every conversation, every piece of evidence, every email—no detail was too small to record. I had become a master of the written word, meticulously chronicling every twist and turn of my insurance battle. If the insurance company dared to challenge my claims, I would unleash the full force of my paperwork arsenal, armed with timestamps, signatures, and enough documentation to rival the Library of Congress.

And just when I thought I had reached my breaking point, a glimmer of hope appeared on the horizon. The insurance company, perhaps sensing my unwavering determination, finally relented. They agreed to cover the damages, albeit begrudgingly. It was a hard-fought victory, one that left me feeling a mix of relief, triumph, and the desire to throw a party with confetti made of insurance paperwork.

So, my fellow adventurers in the land of insurance claims take heart in my tale of dust storms and bureaucratic battles. Remember that you are not alone in this journey. Reach out to fellow landlords, arm yourself with thorough documentation, and never forget to find moments of levity amidst the chaos. Yes, dealing with insurance companies can be a dusty nightmare, but with a dash of humor, a sprinkle of perseverance, and a lot of patience, you'll come out on top, ready to face whatever storms may come your way. And who knows, you might even earn a badge of honor—a dust-covered crown proclaiming you the conqueror of the insurance realm!

Chapter 44:
Hold Tenants Accountable

"I'm Sorry, This Will Never Happen Again... Or Will It?"

Ah, the familiar refrain of "I'm sorry, this will never happen again." It's a line that landlords often hear, accompanied by promises of change and good behavior. But I've learned through years of experience that people don't always change as easily as they claim.

In the world of property management, having zero tolerance for bad behavior is essential. It's a matter of maintaining order, protecting the well-being of other tenants, and preserving the integrity of my property. My mantra is simple: My Property, My Rules. And let me tell you, my friend, I enforce those rules with an iron fist, ready to deliver consequences when they're warranted.

When a tenant breaks one of my rules for the first time, I take immediate action. I note the infraction, documenting the incident as a warning. But I don't stop there. I make sure the tenant knows the gravity of their actions and the potential consequences if it happens again. It's a firm but fair approach, laying the groundwork for accountability and setting clear expectations.

You see, allowing leniency or turning a blind eye to rule-breaking is a slippery slope. If I were to let one tenant get away with breaking the rules, word would spread like wildfire, and soon enough, chaos would reign supreme. It's like dealing with a group of unruly kindergartners, except instead of crayons and nap time, we're dealing with adults and the sanctity of their living spaces.

But here's the thing: sometimes, it feels like a never-ending game of cat and mouse. Some tenants have a knack for pushing boundaries, testing the limits of my patience and resolve. It's as if they see my property as a playground, with rules meant to be bent or broken.

They think they can outsmart me, hide their misdeeds, and continue their disruptive behavior.

Well, my friend, I'm no ordinary landlord. I've developed a sixth sense for sniffing out mischief and catching tenants in the act. Call it intuition or years of experience, but I have an uncanny ability to unearth those hidden infractions. It's like I've become a detective, armed with a magnifying glass and a steely determination to maintain order within my kingdom.

And when I catch them red-handed, I don't hesitate to act. The move-out notice is delivered, and they are left with no choice but to find a new place to call home. It may sound harsh, but it's a necessary measure to protect the integrity of my property and ensure the happiness and safety of other tenants.

You might be thinking, "Is there no room for forgiveness or redemption?" Well, my friend, that's a complicated question. While I believe in giving people a chance to change, actions speak louder than words. If a tenant repeatedly breaks the rules or completely disregards the well-being of others, then it becomes clear that change may be nothing more than an empty promise.

But let's not end on a bleak note. Despite the challenges of dealing with rule-breakers, some tenants respect and appreciate the boundaries I've set. They understand that living in harmony with their neighbors and following the rules leads to a peaceful and pleasant environment. These tenants are the ones who make my job rewarding and remind me why I chose this profession in the first place.

So, my fellow rule enforcers, remember that maintaining order requires vigilance and a steadfast commitment to your principles. Set clear expectations, hold tenants accountable, and don't be afraid to show them the door if necessary.

Chapter 45:
Fool Me Once

"Believe Me, I'm Telling You the Truth, Mr. Landlord!"

Ah, the sweet sound of truth, or so they claim. As a landlord, I've encountered my fair share of tenants who insist their words are the gospel truth. They look me straight in the eye, their expressions earnest, and profess their innocence or provide elaborate explanations for their shortcomings. But after years of experience, I've realized that the truth can be as elusive as a mirage in the desert.

Now, don't get me wrong, my friend. I used to be the most positive person you could imagine. I believed every human being was born innocent, with the best intentions. But as I've grown older and wiser, dealing with countless tenants month after month, that rosy outlook has been chipped away. I've come to understand that cynicism can be a valuable survival tool in property management.

It's a sad truth that most of what comes out of a tenant's mouth is a carefully crafted web of lies. It's almost like they have a Ph.D. in deception. They spin tales to avoid paying fees, to justify late rent payments, or to shirk their responsibilities. It's a never-ending stream of excuses, promises, and elaborate stories designed to manipulate and evade.

In fact, I'm reminded of a quote from the great Judge Judy herself. She once said, "You know when a teenager is lying? When he opens his mouth!" Well, my friend, if we substitute the word "teenager" with "tenant," we have a fitting description of the situation. It seems that honesty is a scarce commodity in the world of rentals.

I don't want to paint all tenants with the same dishonest brush. There are certainly some who are genuine and truthful, and for them, I am eternally grateful. But when it comes to those chronic fibbers and skilled storytellers, well, they keep me on my toes and sometimes even provide a bit of unintentional amusement.

Picture this: a tenant calls me up, claiming that their dog, Fluffy, accidentally ate their rent money. Yes, you heard that right, Fluffy decided to feast on a stack of cash instead of her usual kibble. I have to admit, it's a creative excuse. I can't help but chuckle inside as I listen to their tall tale.

Or how about when a tenant swore they were visited by aliens who zapped their wallet and erased their memory of paying rent? I must say, I've heard my fair share of far-fetched explanations, but this one truly took the cake. During our conversation, I almost expected them to break into a rendition of the X-Files theme song.

But as amusing as these stories may be, they also highlight the need for vigilance. It's like being caught in a game of Truth or Dare, except the tenants always seem to choose "Dare" and dare to fabricate stories that defy logic. It's enough to make you question whether you accidentally stumbled into the Twilight Zone instead of your rental property.

So, how does one navigate this tangled web of deceit? Well, my friend, it all comes down to the art of verification. As a landlord, I've become a master detective, carefully piecing together evidence to separate fact from fiction. I don my metaphorical magnifying glass and investigate with Sherlock Holmes-like precision.

If a tenant claims that they cannot pay a certain fee because they donated their entire paycheck to a charity for talking parrots, I'll politely request some supporting documentation. Maybe a receipt from the parrot charity or a photo of them surrounded by chatty feathered friends. After all, a picture is worth a thousand words, or in this case, a thousand squawks.

I've also learned to trust my instincts, which are often tingling with a sense of skepticism. It's like a sixth sense honed from years of dealing with fibbers and tall-tale tellers. If something sounds too good to be true or too absurd to be believable, chances are it probably is.

But amidst all the deceit, I've also had the pleasure of encountering some genuinely honest and reliable tenants. They're like rays of sunshine on a cloudy day, a refreshing breath of fresh air amidst the sea of excuses. These tenants remind me that not everyone is cut from the same dishonest cloth, and for them, I am grateful.

In conclusion, my fellow landlords, embrace your skepticism, but don't let it dampen your sense of humor. The rental management world can be a wild and unpredictable place, filled with stories that would make even the most seasoned comedians chuckle. Remember to trust your instincts, verify the claims, and keep a straight face while listening to tales of Fluffy's rent-eating adventures.

And who knows, maybe one day we'll compile a book of the most outlandish tenant excuses, giving us all a good laugh and a reminder that truth can be stranger than fiction. After all, in the realm of rentals, laughter is the best antidote to the occasional fib. So, dear landlord, stay vigilant, stay amused, and keep a sturdy magnifying glass handy when the truth seems just a little too elusive.

Chapter 46:
Doing the Right Thing... For the Business

"Why Am I Not Charging Market Rent?"

Ah, the eternal question that haunts the minds of landlords everywhere: why am I not charging market rent? It's a question that requires introspection and a careful evaluation of our business practices. Property owners must constantly review and adjust our rental prices to ensure we're maximizing our profits. After all, running a rental business is not a charity; it's a livelihood.

Sometimes, our hesitation to raise the rent stems from personal reasons. We may have tenants who have been with us for a long time and feel a sense of loyalty or compassion towards them. We know their stories, their adorable children, and we don't want to cause them unnecessary stress by increasing their rent. But as landlords, we must learn to separate our personal feelings from our business decisions.

In this post-COVID period, we're facing an inflation rate that seems to climb higher daily. Costs are rising, from repairs and maintenance to insurance rates. It's a harsh reality that we can't afford to ignore. While donating to worthy causes and supporting organizations like PETA or the American Cancer Society is commendable, we must also prioritize our business success and financial stability.

We are running a business, my friend, not a charity. Each unit we own is a product, and our goal is to maximize the cash flow from every door. It's a delicate balancing act, managing a large property portfolio while ensuring our profits are not compromised. We must adapt to the changing market conditions and adjust our rental prices accordingly.

Now, you may wonder, "But what about the tenants? Won't they try to skip out on paying rent or move out without notice if I raise the rent?" Ah, you've hit the nail on the head. Everyone is looking out for number one, and it's only natural that tenants will prioritize their financial well-being. As savvy landlords, it's up to us to protect our interests and ensure that our business thrives.

Raising the rent is not an act of cruelty or greed; it's a necessary step to maintain the viability of our rental business. We must cover our increasing costs, preserve profitability, and secure our livelihood. It's a matter of survival in an ever-changing economic landscape.

But fear not, my fellow landlords, for there is a silver lining. Increasing the rent doesn't mean we have to abandon all sense of fairness and empathy. We can still communicate with our tenants, explain the reasons behind the rent increase, and offer transparency in our business dealings. We can build trust and maintain positive relationships with our tenants by fostering open and honest communication.

So, my dear landlord, ask yourself, "Why am I not charging market rent?" Evaluate your business practices, assess the market conditions, and make the necessary adjustments. Remember, mercy may be for the meek, but maximizing cash flow is for the determined and successful. Raise that rent with confidence, my friend, and secure the future of your rental empire.

In the end, we are not just landlords; we are entrepreneurs, visionaries, and masters of our own destiny. So go forth, my fellow landlords, and may your rental business thrive as you navigate the ever-changing currents of the real estate world.

Chapter 47:
"The Bathtub Battle"

Ah, the joys of being a landlord. Dealing with tenant requests and complaints is an inevitable part of our job. But occasionally, we encounter a tenant who pushes the limits, demanding unnecessary upgrades or replacements. Such was the case with a tenant who insisted on getting a new bathtub.

Now, let me set the record straight. The bathtub in question was not in disrepair or malfunctioning. It had simply endured the wear and tear that naturally occurs over time. And who was responsible for this wear and tear? None other than the very tenant making the demands!

When faced with such audacity, I decided to take a firm stance. I refused to entertain the tenant's unreasonable request. Instead, I calmly informed him that if he felt the need to move out over a perfectly functional bathtub, he was free to do so. It was a bold move but one that needed to be made. I had reached my limit with his constant complaints and endless requests.

To my surprise, my response seemed to put him in his place. Suddenly, the tenant's demands quieted, and I felt a newfound peace. He realized that I was not someone to be trifled with, and the threats of moving out faded into the background. From then on, he became one of my good tenants, causing minimal trouble and offering no further complaints.

Moments like these remind me of the importance of standing our ground as landlords. We must assert ourselves and establish boundaries to control our properties and sanity. No amount of money or tenant drama is worth sacrificing our time and well-being.

As landlords, we can choose who we want to rent to and who we'd rather not have as tenants. Remembering that we hold the keys to our success and happiness in this business is important. If someone proves to be more trouble than they're worth, it's perfectly acceptable to bid them farewell and let them become someone else's problem.

In the end, our time and health are valuable assets that we must protect. We cannot allow ourselves to be constantly at the beck and call of demanding tenants. By setting boundaries and asserting our authority, we create an environment where tenants understand we are not to be taken advantage of.

So, fellow landlords, let us stand strong and firm in the face of unreasonable demands. Let us prioritize our well-being and the smooth operation of our rental business. And may we always remember that it's perfectly fine to bid farewell to troublesome tenants and seek greener pastures. After all, plenty of good tenants out there will respect our properties and make our lives as landlords much more enjoyable.

Chapter 48:
To Patch or Replace?

As landlords, we often face the dilemma of whether to patch up a broken element in our property or go ahead and replace it entirely. It's a decision that requires careful consideration as we strive to balance maximizing profit and improving our properties.

When it comes to urgent matters like air conditioning or plumbing issues, there's no question that they should be treated as emergencies and addressed immediately. But what about improvements to the property? How do we determine whether it's worth investing in a quick patch or opting for a full replacement?

I've grappled with this question myself over the years, and while I don't claim to have all the answers, I've developed a rule of thumb that guides my decision-making process. If the money spent on a particular improvement will yield a return on investment within five years, then it's likely worth pursuing. This return on investment can come in various forms, such as attracting more potential tenants or increasing the property's resale value.

Every penny spent on property improvements should have a clear return on investment, or else it risks being wasted. And trust me, those pennies can add up over time. As landlords, it's our responsibility to ensure that every expenditure contributes to our properties' overall profitability and desirability.

In addition to the return on investment consideration, I follow some additional rules when deciding whether to replace or repair items in my properties. Firstly, I only replace items under two conditions: when it's a profitable upgrade that allows me to charge higher rent after the improvement or when replacing the item is more cost-effective than repairing it. These rules help me make sound financial decisions that align with the long-term success of my rental business.

When prioritizing upgrades, I've found that focusing on the kitchen and bathroom tends to yield the best return on investment. These areas are often considered the heart of a home, and tenants are willing to pay a premium for modern, well-maintained spaces in these rooms. By investing in upgrades and renovations in these key areas, I can attract higher-quality tenants and potentially increase rental income.

Of course, every property and situation are unique, and there may be exceptions to these general guidelines. It's important to assess each situation on a case-by-case basis, considering factors such as the property's location, market demand, and overall condition.

Finding the right balance between profitability and property improvement is an ongoing challenge for landlords. It requires careful evaluation, financial foresight, and a clear understanding of the local rental market. By following a set of guidelines, weighing the potential return on investment, and prioritizing upgrades in key areas, we can make informed decisions that enhance the value of our properties and ensure long-term success in the rental business.

Remember, as landlords, we are not only in the business of providing shelter but also in the business of making sound financial investments. By approaching property improvements strategically, we can create spaces that attract tenants, maximize profitability, and ultimately build a thriving rental business.

Chapter 49:
Turning Mistakes into Learning Opportunities

In my journey as a landlord, I've encountered countless experiences and made my fair share of mistakes. But instead of dwelling on my errors, I've chosen to embrace them as valuable learning opportunities. Each misstep has served as a lesson that has shaped my approach to property management and allowed me to become a better landlord.

When I find myself in a situation where I've made a mistake, I resist the temptation to beat myself up over it. Instead, I step back and thoroughly analyze the entire scenario. I reflect on why I made my choices and explore ways to improve my decision-making process for future reference. By conducting this self-reflection, I can uncover valuable insights that help me avoid repeating the same mistakes.

Taking notes on my mistakes and downfalls has become an essential practice in my journey as a landlord. I document the details of each situation, including what went wrong, what factors contributed to the mistake, and the potential consequences. These notes serve as a reminder and reference point, ensuring I don't forget the valuable lessons I've learned. Reviewing these notes periodically helps me reinforce those lessons and stay vigilant in my decision-making.

However, the value of these lessons extends beyond the realm of business. Mistakes provide an opportunity for personal growth and self-improvement. They teach us humility, resilience, and the importance of continuous learning. By embracing our mistakes and using them as steppingstones, we can become better versions of ourselves as landlords and individuals.

It's important to remember that mistakes are a natural part of life, and no one is immune to them. Instead of fearing mistakes or viewing them as failures, we should embrace them as opportunities for growth. Each mistake carries a wealth of knowledge and experience that can propel us forward on our journey.

By acknowledging our mistakes and actively seeking to learn from them, we demonstrate a commitment to personal and professional development. We become more adept at navigating the challenges of being a landlord and are better equipped to handle similar situations in the future.

So, my fellow landlords, let's not waste a single mistake. Instead, let's approach them with a mindset of curiosity and self-improvement. Take the time to reflect, analyze, and document the valuable lessons learned. By doing so, we transform our mistakes into opportunities for growth and pave the way for a successful and fulfilling journey as landlords.

Remember, the path to success is not a straight line but a series of twists and turns. Embrace the bumps along the way, for they hold the keys to our growth and transformation.

Chapter 50:
When to Step In

"It's late, turn that loud music off!"

Ah, the sweet symphony of neighborly disputes. As a landlord, I've had my fair share of complaints about loud music echoing through the hallways. It's a delicate situation that requires a careful approach. So, when a tenant comes knocking on my door, demanding that I do something about their noisy neighbor, I take a moment to assess the situation and consider the best course of action.

Now, let's be honest. Regarding tenant complaints, it's always a toss-up whether they're telling the truth or not. Not to sound cynical, but tenants sometimes have their own motives when accusing their neighbors of violations. They might be trying to get their neighbor in trouble or seek revenge for perceived wrongdoing. So, I take their complaints with a grain of salt and approach the situation with a healthy dose of skepticism.

Picture this: a tenant storms into my office, fuming about the neighbor's loud music. They're waving their hands in the air, demonstrating just how high the volume was. I can't help but wonder if they've been practicing their conductor skills while I was busy managing the property. Moments like these make you question whether you've accidentally stumbled into a neighborhood drama series instead of being a landlord.

Instead of immediately donning my superhero cape and rushing to the rescue, I encourage my tenants to resolve minor issues among themselves. I become the mediator, urging them to knock on their neighbor's door and kindly ask them to lower the volume of their music. After all, a polite conversation can work wonders. I reassure the complaining tenant, saying, "I'm sure your neighbor is reasonable. Just ask them nicely if they could turn down the music while you're trying to get some sleep."

But let me tell you, my fellow landlords, sometimes the stories I hear from tenants about their neighbors' behavior are enough to make your head spin. I once had a tenant claim that their neighbor's taste in music was so atrocious that it caused their pet parrot to start squawking along in protest. They insisted it was a form of avian torture and demanded immediate action. As much as I empathized with their feathered friend, I had to remind them that parrot karaoke disputes were outside my realm of expertise.

You see, I'm not a judge, nor do I want to be caught in the crossfire of a nasty back-and-forth between tenants. It's a recipe for disaster and unnecessary headaches. I strive to maintain a neutral position, avoiding taking sides and creating further tension within the community. It's like walking a tightrope, balancing the needs and interests of my tenants while preserving a sense of harmony.

However, there comes a point when multiple tenants start complaining about the same issue. When the chorus of discontent grows louder, it's a clear sign that action must be taken. If I receive multiple complaints about a particular tenant's disruptive behavior, it becomes a problem that needs immediate attention. After all, I can't afford to lose tenants over constant disturbances.

In such cases, I step in and address the issue head-on. I contact the tenant causing the disturbance and have a frank conversation about the noise levels and its impact on the community. I remind them of the importance of being considerate and respectful towards their neighbors. Sometimes a friendly reminder is all they need to adjust their behavior and keep the peace.

But let's not forget, my dear fellow landlords, that we are not miracle workers. We can't control every aspect of our tenants' lives. We can set guidelines and enforce rules, but we can't micromanage their every action. So finding the right balance between direct involvement and stepping back is crucial. This approach allows tenants to address the issue amongst themselves and reach a resolution effectively.

Chapter 51:
DIY vs Property Management Company

"Why are you charging me $400 when it should only cost no more than $120?"

Ah, the allure of outsourcing. Many landlords have contemplated the idea of handing over the reins to a property management company, hoping to free up their time and alleviate the burdens of tenant management. However, my dear landlord comrades, I stand firmly against this notion. I believe in managing my properties myself and let me tell you why.

First and foremost, let's talk about the elephant in the room: cost. Property management companies often charge a hefty fee for their services, which can add up faster than a runaway utility bill. I've heard stories of landlords being charged exorbitant amounts for simple repairs and maintenance tasks. Why pay $1000 to replace a toilet when I can hire a skilled handyman to do the job for a fraction of the cost? It's like trying to fix a leaky faucet by hiring a plumber with a penchant for gold-plated wrenches—it simply doesn't make financial sense.

You see, my fellow landlords, property management companies are businesses too. And like any business, their primary goal is to maximize profits. While I can't fault them for their intentions, it doesn't align with my vision for my rental business. I want to minimize expenses and maximize my returns. By managing my properties myself, I have more control over the costs associated with repairs, maintenance, and other day-to-day operations. I can carefully choose reliable and cost-effective contractors, ensuring that I get the best value for my money.

Furthermore, managing tenants myself allows me to maintain a personal touch and a direct line of communication. When issues arise, I can address them promptly and effectively. I become the point person for all tenant concerns, building relationships based on trust and understanding. After all, who knows my tenants better than I do? I have firsthand knowledge of their needs, preferences, and quirks. It's like being the conductor of a well-rehearsed orchestra, ensuring that all the instruments are in tune and playing harmoniously.

But it's not just about financial savings and personal connections. Managing my properties myself gives me a sense of pride and ownership. I take responsibility for every decision and action, knowing that success or failure rests squarely on my shoulders. There's a sense of empowerment in knowing that I can shape the destiny of my rental business. If I make a mistake, there's no one else to blame but myself. But when I succeed, the rewards are all mine to savor. It's like hitting the jackpot in the landlord lottery, where every dollar earned is a testament to my skills and expertise.

Of course, I won't deny that managing properties can be time-consuming and challenging. It requires dedication, organization, and the ability to juggle multiple responsibilities. But isn't that the case with any business endeavor? It's a labor of love, a journey that tests your mettle and rewards your perseverance. And let's not forget the joy of witnessing the growth of your investment, seeing your properties thrive under your careful guidance.

Ah, the world of property management, where the decisions we make can have a significant impact on our investments. As I navigate this realm, a thought often crosses my mind: "Is hiring a property management company really the best choice?" Let me take you on a personal journey filled with insights and revelations as I share my experiences and ponder the pros and cons of relying on these companies to manage my properties.

In the world of property management, it is common to encounter minimum 12-month agreements. This means that once I've signed on the dotted line, I am bound to the property management company for the entirety of that period. If I am dissatisfied with their services or feel that they are not meeting my expectations, I must endure the entire 12-month duration before I can make a change. And let me tell you, dear reader, that doesn't sound like a fair deal to me.

As I reflect on this predicament, I yearn for a different arrangement—a setup where I have more control and the ability to terminate a service provider at any time if they fail to deliver. After all, isn't it empowering to have someone who reports directly to me, someone who is accountable for their actions and performance? The thought of making swift decisions and taking immediate action brings a sense of relief and peace of mind.

Furthermore, it's important to recognize that property management companies don't always have our best interests at heart. Their primary goal is not to maximize our net profit but to make money for themselves. This misalignment of interests can lead to situations where they prioritize their financial gains over our bottom line. An example that often makes me cringe is their exorbitant fees for seemingly simple tasks. Take, for instance, the replacement of a toilet. A property management company might charge a staggering $400, whereas I know I can easily hire a handyman to do the job for less than $120. The margin they're making off of me is astounding and, frankly, hard to swallow.

In this personal journey of reflection, I'm reminded of the importance of weighing the pros and cons and making choices that align with my values and objectives. While property management companies can offer convenience and expertise in certain areas, it's crucial to remain vigilant and critically evaluate the value they bring to our investment endeavors.

So, my friends, as we navigate the complex landscape of property management, let us ponder the alternatives and consider whether taking matters into our own hands is the right path for us. Remember, we have the power to shape our destinies as property owners, and sometimes that means forging our path to success.

So, my dear landlords, before you consider relinquishing control to a property management company, consider the potential drawbacks and the missed opportunities. Remember that you are not just a landlord; you are an entrepreneur with a vision. With the right systems, mindset, and a dash of DIY spirit, you can run your rental business efficiently and profitably. Embrace the challenges, learn from your mistakes, and revel in the rewards of being the captain of your own landlord ship.

In conclusion, my friends, managing my properties myself allows me to save costs, maintain direct communication with tenants, and take pride in my achievements. It's a winning strategy that aligns with my goals and keeps me in control of my destiny. So, let's raise a glass to the DIY landlords, the masters of their rental domains, and let the property management companies handle someone else's plumbing woes.

Chapter 52:
The Golden Rule

"Whoever has the gold makes the rules."

I've realized that being a landlord requires a certain level of mental toughness. It's a tough world in the rental business and one needs to have a resilient mindset to navigate the challenges that come with it. Timid individuals would find it difficult to survive in this industry, as tenants can often be relentless in pushing boundaries and breaking rules. Alongside the multitude of tasks that landlords must handle, there is an additional layer of tenant drama that can be overwhelming at times, both physically and mentally.

Fortunately, when I first embarked on this journey as a landlord, I was fortunate to have a mentor who guided me through the ups and downs of the business. The advice they imparted to me has been invaluable, and I would like to share it with you. The first piece of wisdom they shared was never to allow myself to be intimidated or disrespected by any tenant. They emphasized that this is a dog-eat-dog world, and to survive, I must develop a tough exterior. This doesn't mean being harsh or unkind, but rather standing firm in my position and not allowing others to take advantage of me. I always have a landlord attorney on retainer to ensure that I am always protected legally and doing the right thing. This gives me the necessary legal coverage and peace of mind in case any tenant-related issues arise.

The second lesson I learned was the importance of understanding that I hold all the leverage as the landlord. There's a saying that goes, "Whoever has the gold makes the rules," and it holds true in this context. If I don't run my property with a firm grip, ruthless tenants will take the opportunity to run amok and trample over both me and my property. Therefore, I must assert my authority and maintain control over the property, upholding rules and regulations.

However, the most important lesson my mentor taught me was remembering that difficult times shall pass. No matter how challenging or overwhelming a situation may seem, it is temporary, and I will move forward. This perspective has been a saving grace for me during tough times. Instead of getting bogged down by the difficulties, I try to find the humor in them. Laughter truly is the best medicine, and by looking at the positive or funny side of things, I can let go and find happiness amidst the chaos.

Now, let's dive into some real-life stories highlighting the trials and tribulations I've faced as a landlord. These stories underscore the challenges I've encountered and remind me that humor can be found even in the most exasperating situations.

One memorable incident involved a tenant who seemed determined to test my limits. They constantly pushed the boundaries, breaking every rule in the book. This tenant was the epitome of trouble, from unauthorized pets to disruptive behavior that disturbed the neighbors. I found myself constantly addressing their infractions and issuing warnings. However, despite my best efforts, they seemed unfazed and continued to push the envelope.

I decided to have a heart-to-heart conversation with the tenant to address the situation. As I approached their door, armed with determination and trepidation, I was greeted by an unexpected sight. The tenant opened the door with a mischievous grin, holding a fake eviction notice they had made as a prank. I couldn't help but chuckle at their audacity and creativity at that moment. While their actions were unacceptable, I couldn't deny the sheer audacity of their prank. It reminded us that sometimes, even amidst the chaos, we can find amusement in unexpected places.

Another incident involved a tenant with an incessant need for attention. They would constantly call, email, and visit the property office with a barrage of questions and complaints, demanding immediate resolution to the most trivial matters. As I tried to balance their needs with the demands of other tenants and my responsibilities, I often felt like a spinning top, struggling to keep up with their demands.

One day, I received a call from the tenant with yet another list of complaints. I patiently listened as they vented their frustrations about every minute detail, from a squeaky door hinge to the color of the walls. While their concerns were valid to some extent, the sheer volume of issues left me feeling overwhelmed. In sheer spontaneity, I responded with a touch of sarcasm, saying, "Well, it seems like you're on a roll today! How about we organize a Tenant Olympics? You can go for gold in the 'Complaining about Everything' category!" To my surprise, the tenant burst into laughter, acknowledging the situation's absurdity. From that day forward, our interactions were lighter, and their demands became more reasonable.

These anecdotes serve as reminders that amidst the trials and tribulations of being a landlord, maintaining a sense of humor can be a powerful tool. By finding the funny side of things, I can diffuse tension, ease stress, and ultimately maintain a positive outlook. While the challenges may be daunting at times, I approach them with a lighthearted perspective, knowing that laughter is a valuable asset in navigating the unpredictable world of property management.

In conclusion, the journey of a landlord is not for the faint of heart. It requires mental toughness, resilience, and a healthy dose of humor. By heeding the advice of my mentor, understanding my leverage as a landlord, and embracing the notion that difficult times shall pass, I can face the trials and tribulations of this profession with grace and a smile. Through amusing anecdotes and valuable life lessons, I have shared my experiences as a landlord, highlighting the importance of maintaining a sense of humor and perspective. So, my fellow landlords, let us forge ahead with confidence, armed with laughter and a firm grip on the challenges that come our way. Together, we can navigate the rental world with resilience, tenacity, and a hearty laugh.

Chapter 53:
Conclusion - Embracing the Landlord Life

"A Journey of Freedom and Prosperity."

As we come to the end of this book, I want to take a moment to celebrate the many positives of being a landlord. It's a career path that offers financial rewards and a unique sense of freedom and fulfillment. So, let's raise our glasses one final time and toast to the incredible journey of being a landlord.

One of the greatest advantages of being a landlord is the freedom it provides. While it's true that managing properties comes with its fair share of responsibilities, it also offers flexibility and the ability to control your own time. Unlike the constraints of a traditional 9-to-5 job, as a landlord, you can set your schedule, work at your own pace, and enjoy a level of independence that few other careers can offer. Whether it's taking a well-deserved vacation or spending quality time with loved ones, being a landlord allows you to prioritize what truly matters to you.

But the benefits don't end there. Let's talk about the financial side of things. Being a landlord presents a tremendous opportunity to build wealth and achieve financial prosperity. With each property you add to your portfolio, you create a new income stream and increase your potential for long-term growth. The rental income generated from your properties can provide a stable and consistent cash flow, allowing you to pursue your dreams and live on your terms.

Moreover, real estate has historically proven to be a solid investment that can appreciate over time. As a landlord, you can build property equity, benefiting from rental income and property appreciation. This combination can lead to significant wealth accumulation and open doors to further investment opportunities. The possibilities are endless, and with careful planning and strategy, the sky's the limit.

Beyond financial gains, being a landlord allows you to positively impact people's lives. You become an integral part of their journey by providing safe and comfortable homes for tenants. You can create a nurturing environment where individuals and families can thrive. The satisfaction of knowing that you are playing a role in shaping the lives of others is immeasurable. From first-time renters to long-term tenants, your efforts as a landlord contribute to the fabric of a community and foster a sense of belonging for those who call your properties home.

Let's not forget the opportunities for personal growth from being a landlord. The challenges you face—dealing with difficult tenants, managing repairs, navigating legal requirements—push you to expand your knowledge and develop valuable skills. You become a master of negotiation, problem-solving, and effective communication. Each hurdle you overcome strengthens your resilience and equips you with the tools to tackle any obstacle that comes your way. As a landlord, you are not just a caretaker of properties but a lifelong learner, constantly evolving and improving in both your personal and professional capacities.

In conclusion, being a landlord is a journey filled with freedom, financial abundance, and personal growth. It's a career that allows you to shape your destiny, create a legacy, and enjoy the fruits of your labor. So, my fellow landlords, let's celebrate the joys of our chosen path—the sense of freedom, the potential for financial prosperity, and the opportunity to make a positive impact in the lives of others. Embrace the challenges, savor the successes, and continue building your empire, one property at a time. Cheers to the incredible journey of being a landlord!

Epilogue:

If you find yourself hungry for more landlord success stories and eager to uncover further strategies for managing your rental empire with ease, then I invite you to dive into my first book, "Millionaire Landlord Secrets: Hacks & tips on how to manage 100+ rental properties working 4 hours a week!" It's a treasure trove of knowledge and inspiration that will help you unlock the secrets to running a thriving rental business while reclaiming your precious time.

You can easily purchase "Millionaire Landlord Secrets" on Amazon by following the link below. I assure you the investment in this book will be a game-changer for your landlord journey, empowering you to achieve financial abundance and personal freedom.

Purchase "Millionaire Landlord Secrets" on Amazon:

https://tinyurl.com/MillionaireLandlordSecrets

But here's the icing on the cake—I would be incredibly grateful if you could take a moment to share your thoughts and experiences by leaving a review on Amazon. Your feedback is not only valuable to me, but it will also guide other aspiring landlords on their path to success. By leaving a positive review, you'll be making a meaningful contribution to the community of landlords seeking knowledge and inspiration.

Thank you from the bottom of my heart for your support and joining me on this thrilling adventure. Together, we can conquer the challenges of landlording and create a vibrant community of successful landlords. So, grab a copy of "Millionaire Landlord Secrets" and embark on a journey that will forever transform your rental business.

Happy reading, and may your rental empire soar to new heights!

P.S. Don't forget to leave a review on Amazon! Your feedback is invaluable and greatly appreciated.

About the Author

Introducing Jason A. Scott, a highly accomplished entrepreneur, author, private pilot, world traveler, and real estate investor with an extensive portfolio of over 100 rental units. With a career in real estate dating back to 2009, he has honed his expertise in property management and utilized a successful Buy & Hold strategy, resulting in his remarkable achievement of becoming a decamillionaire by the age of 45.

As a business consultant and life coach, Jason has empowered numerous individuals to realize extraordinary results through self-discipline and persistent focus. He has conducted inspiring seminars, showcasing the power of real estate investing and the path to financial freedom. In addition to his latest book, Jason has authored two other highly acclaimed works:

1. "Millionaire Landlord Secrets" - Discover invaluable insights into the world of real estate investing.

https://tinyurl.com/MillionaireLandlordSecrets

2. "Millionaire Success Secrets" - Unlock the secrets to achieve success and prosperity in life and business.

https://tinyurl.com/MillionaireSuccessSecrets

Beyond his professional endeavors, Jason embraces a life of adventure, indulging in his passion for flying and nurturing his homes across Asia, Europe, and the United States.

Book Recommendation

Here are 10 recommended books on tenant management that can help landlords improve their skills and navigate the challenges of property management:

1. "The Landlord's Kit: A Complete Set of Ready-to-Use Forms, Letters, and Notices to Increase Profits, Take Control, and Eliminate Hassles" by Jeffrey Taylor

2. "The Book on Managing Rental Properties: A Proven System for Finding, Screening, and Managing Tenants with Fewer Headaches and Maximum Profit" by Brandon Turner and Heather Turner

3. "The Complete Landlord and Property Manager's Legal Survival Kit" by Diana Brodman Summers

4. "Every Landlord's Guide to Managing Property: Best Practices, From Move-In to Move-Out" by Michael Boyer Attorney and Janet Portman Attorney

5. "The Landlord Entrepreneur: Double Your Profits with Real Estate Property Management" by Bryan M. Chavis

6. "Property Management Kit For Dummies" by Robert S. Griswold

7. "The Property Management Tool Kit" by Mike Beirne

8. "The Landlord's Legal Guide in California" by Ralph Warner, Janet Portman, and David Brown

9. "The Successful Landlord: How to Make Money Without Making Yourself Nuts" by Ken Roth

10. "Landlording on AutoPilot: A Simple, No-Brainer System for Higher Profits, Less Work and More Fun (Do It All from Your Smartphone or Tablet!)" by Mike Butler

These books cover a wide range of topics related to tenant management, including tenant screening, legal considerations, maintenance and repairs, and maximizing profitability. Each offers valuable insights and practical advice to help landlords manage their properties effectively and build successful rental businesses. Happy reading!